Symphony on Fire

A Story of Music and Spiritual Resistance During the Holocaust

Sonia Pauline Beker

The Wordsmithy, LLC
New Milford, NJ

Symphony on Fire:
A Story of Music and Spiritual
Resistance During the Holocaust

Copyright© 2007 by Sonia Pauline Beker
ISBN 0-9748857-5-4

Cover design by Brian Retchless
BC Graphics/Media Technology Services
in association with Etoile International Productions

Published by The Wordsmithy, LLC
PO Box 224
New Milford, NJ 07646
1-800-780-5183
www.the wordsmithy.com

Library of Congress Cataloging-in-Publication Data
Beker, Sonia Pauline
Symphony on Fire: A Story of Music and Spiritual Resistance
During the Holocaust
        p. cm.
ISBN 0-9748857-5-4
1. Max Beker. 2. Fania Durmashkin-Beker 3. Jews–Lithuania–
Vilnius (Vilna)–Biography 4. Jewish musicians 5. Concentration
camp inmates–music. 6. Holocaust, Jewish (1939-1945)–personal
narratives. 7. Holocaust survivors.

TABLE OF CONTENTS

DEDICATION

To my parents, Fania Durmashkin-Beker and Max Beker.
To the memory of the Durmashkin and Beker families, may their
sweet souls also have a place in this world with this book.
To the souls of Vilna's 80,000 lost Jews.
To the Six Million.

May the world one day wake up and be ruled by true compassion,
respect and celebration of human diversity.

ACKNOWLEDGMENTS

This book is a living memoir. It reminds us to appreciate how blessed we are when our loved ones are with us in this world, and how richly they continue to bless us after they pass on. Writing it was a privilege, working on it, a revelation. As I delved more deeply into my parents' lives and their histories, into the many photos and documents they left behind (because they were people who did not easily discard their past), they became the keys to hidden treasures, discoveries more precious than rubies. For this, immense gratitude and acknowledgements go to my parents, their families, friends, and the Vilna Jewish community as it existed at its cultural zenith before the war, and as it exists now—full of warmth, love, spunk, hope, courage, cohesiveness, differences of opinion, and deep respect for its venerable past.

As I learned more about my parents' lives in pre-war Vilna, and the roles they played in the Vilna ghetto, I found I had a paucity of information about their lives in the post-war period. I knew about my father's fate as a Nazi-captured POW, and about my mother who lived through Dachau, but how did my parents, as well as all the other survivors who came up for air in DP camps after the war, embrace life again and adjust to a new world?

Years ago—at my request—they had both written their memoirs and strangely, both stopped writing at the same point—their respective liberations—as if the story ended there.

To find out what happened, I called a close, old family friend, Jascha Gurewitz, who'd been the manager of the St. Ottilien Jewish Orchestra and the Ex-Concentration Camp Orchestra. I thank him for his generous friendship, his sensitive heart, and his inspiring resilience as a survivor. Jascha agreed to be interviewed and was helpful in providing more information about how the orchestra was formed. He graciously gave me several astonishing documents—programs of the orchestra's performances in Munich and Nuremberg, including the two performances Leonard Bernstein conducted.

There was also an invitation to a film screening that had taken place several years earlier in New Jersey. The film was entitled *Displaced: Miracle at St. Ottilien*, the story of two American GIs, Edward Herman and Robert Hilliard, who were stationed at the St. Ottilien DP Camp. They discovered that the Jewish survivors, in the camp run by the American military, were being treated horrendously while Nazi officers, also inmates, were getting royal treatment. To alleviate the survivors' suffering, Herman and Hilliard stole food from their own mess hall and smuggled it into the camp. They also began a massive letter-writing campaign across America to try to get help for the Jewish DPs.

The film was based on *Surviving the Americans: The Continued Struggle of the Jews After Liberation*, a book by Robert Hilliard, the same American GI who later became a journalist. I ordered copies of the book and film, found the name of the filmmaker, John Michalczyk, and called him in Boston. I asked him the question I dreaded to ask, "John, are Edward Herman or Robert Hilliard still alive?" "Alive!" he replied. "They are so alive, they make me feel tired!" Both travel the country giving lectures.

Once I found him, Ed Herman graciously invited me and my significant other, Steve Zucker, to his home in Florida. Ed also invited the St. Ottilien "family"—friends he'd kept in touch with from the DP camp, including some children of survivors who were born there. I brought along many St. Ottilien photographs and a couple of newsletters to share with the group, and, as Steve filmed the gathering in Ed's living room, there was a great deal of storytelling, and nostalgic recollections were generated. Inspired by our get-together, the work on my book and the materials we viewed, Ed contacted John and told him that he just had to make a film about the orchestra. And so, the film, *Creating Harmony: The Displaced Persons Orchestra at St. Ottilien*, was born.

Thank you, Ed Herman, for your sensitive, clear vision, your golden heart and your uncanny, can-do attitude. You've been a champion of our people, correcting injustice all your life. Your loving kindness and support mean the world to me. Thank you, John Michalczyk and Etoile International Productions, for your generous heart and spirit, your outstanding talent, your willingness to take risks for what is truly worthwhile—and for your infinite patience. Robert Hilliard, thank you for your excellent book. Unable to put it down, I read it in one sitting, all through the night, often in tears.

The next phase of this remarkable journey took me to Vilna—Vilnius, Lithuania—my parents' home city. My time in Vilnius would not have been nearly as full or as fruitful without my talented friend, Marija Krupoves. Thank you, Marija, *mein shwesterel* (my little sister), for making the rough edges smooth, for handing me the keys to so many doors and introducing me to such outstanding people in the precious Vilna Jewish community. You're a beloved teacher, singer, and historian in your own right, much loved for your graciousness and goodness.

Through Marija, I met the following unforgettable Vilnaites. In November 1999, Pranas Morkus sent me a letter telling me a remarkable story. Pranas, you introduced yourself as a Lithuanian Vilnaite who, one day while browsing through a bookstore in the Old Town, came across a volume about the Vilna Ghetto. In it you read about Wolf Durmashkin, his extraordinary musical

Invitation to Pranas Morkus' Vilna Ghetto concert
memorializing Wolf Durmashkin.

achievments and his bitter end. So moved by Wolf's short life, you decided to create a memorial concert in his name in the Ghetto Theater where Wolf had performed during those desperate years. The concert was held and recorded on August 19, 1999. Thank you, Pranas, for your sensitive intellect, your generous heart and respect for great talent. Because you made the concert and the CD in his memory, his name remains alive and connected to music in the city which once applauded him and tossed flowers at his feet on the stage of the Vilna Philharmonic.

Rachel Kostanian, deputy director of the Vilna Gaon State Jewish Museum, is a talented writer and a deeply sensitive, caring guardian of the history of Vilna's Jews. Thank you, Rachel, for taking your valuable time to show me the archives at the Jewish museums under your care and supervision in the city. Your book, *Spiritual Resistance in the Vilna Ghetto*, is a tender, moving, and scholarly tribute to those who rose so high, and were then so cruelly taken from us.

Roza Bieliauskiene, chief curator of the Vilna Gaon Jewish State Museum, is a tireless champion and keeper of the valuable artifacts in the museum, and the tender souls—teachers, students, and administrators—who used those artifacts right there within the museum walls in what was once the Tarbut Hebrew Gymnasium. Thank you for spending so much time with me to explain, to translate, and to copy documents. Your quiet dedication and deep love for your work and community touched me very deeply.

To Professor Dovid Katz, a special thank you. You are a brilliant scholar, who is much loved by the Jewish community and beyond for all the *mitzvahs* (good deeds) you do for others. Thank you for being an inspiration in academia and especially in the loving kindness you show the Jewish elderly you constantly care for. Thank you for your lively, erudite evening talks in the cafes and restaurants we frequented, and for making me laugh until I cried.

Dr. and Mrs. Markas Petuchauskas, thank you for keeping the flame of memory alight for the souls of the artists, musicians, writers, and educators of pre-war Vilna and its ghetto. By continuing to write and publish articles about their work, you make them live. Thank you especially, Mrs. Petuchauskas, for saying about my uncle, Wolf Durmashkin, "You see? For us, he is still alive."

Judith Rozina, academic associate of the Vilna Gaon Jewish State Museum, thank you for taking extra time to familiarize me with your current projects at the Museum, for your wisdom and dedication, and for welcoming me so warmly.

Ruta Puisyte, assistant director of the Vilnius University Yiddish Institute, thank you for your warmth and concern, for being so helpful and supportive, and for that wonderful cup of mint tea and conversation. The Institute is so lucky to have you on staff.

Khasia Shpanerflik, thank you for spending time sharing your memories of my mother when you were both students, and for the stories of my Uncle Wolf, when you sang in his ghetto choir.

Regina Kopilevich, Jewish Vilna guide and genealogist, thank you for your effervescence, intelligence, and high energy. In the journeys we made under your guidance, your courtesy and courage opened doors whose thresholds I never would have crossed alone.

Stefan Lushkevich, Jewish Vilna guide, thank you for your generosity, your kindness, and gallantry. Your sensitivity, gentlemanly spirit, and breadth of knowledge taught me so much, and added much more to the journey.

Benyamin Anolik, general director of the Janusz Korczak Association at the Ghetto Fighters House in Israel, thank you for sharing your Klooga camp experiences, especially your thoughts about what might have been Wolf Durmashkin's last moments there. Your enthusiasm for life and your mission to disseminate the truth are a true inspiration.

To the members of the Vilna Jewish Community, thank you for graciously including me in your invitation to attend Dovid Katz's birthday celebration, which, in turn, led to my being interviewed for the Menorah TV program. Your work for Vilna's Jews is extremely important.

Thank you Rabbi and Mrs. Krinsky for valiantly bringing back a religious Jewish community to Vilna. I will never forget your kindness and hospitality to me and so many others on *Shabbos* (the Jewish Sabbath). Thank you, Rabbi Feffer, for your *Shabbos* hospitality as well, and for your role at the Chorale Synagogue.

Mira Van Doren, filmmaker and Vilna authority, thank you for honoring my family by including them in your excellent film, *The World Was Ours*, about pre-war cultural Jewish Vilna. Thank you, too, for sharing your opinions, knowledge, and true appreciation of that culture, and the endlessly fascinating artistic individuals who flourished there all too briefly.

Thank you, Regina Sieradski, for graciously and fluently translating my parents' writings with me. You kindly opened your home on good days and difficult ones to make it possible for me to proceed with this book and have meaningful visits with you. Also thank you Lazer Mishulovin for your efforts in translating my parents' Yiddish into English and Richard Radu for German translation.

To Deborah Ehrenberg, thank you for your grace and patience, translating correspondence from French to English while deftly ministering to your lovely children.

Thank you, Cheryl Holder, for your kind care of my father until the end, and your gentle support as we so painfully dismantled my parents' house and our lives as a family.

My many thanks to Faye Ran for granting me the right to use material from the collection of her father, Leyzer Ran (1911-1995), distinguished writer, scholar and cultural historian who devoted his life to Yiddish culture and the legacy of Jewish Vilna. The photos on pages 75 and 94 may also be seen in Leyzer Ran's book, *Jerusalem of Lithuania* (New York: The Laureate Press, 1974).

Thank you, Rabbi and Shternie Raskin and the Raskin kids, for bolstering my spirit all these years—especially when my parents were gone and while this book was in progress.

My deep gratitude to B'nai Avraham and all my good friends there who have become my family over the years. You have given me the most precious gifts of all—love, support, and friendship, the best that life and God have to offer.

Jeanette Friedman, my editor, thank you for your feisty wisdom and fearlessness. You will take any risk to promote what you believe is right and true, especially as it relates to the Holocaust and our survivors. Thanks for so skillfully polishing my words until they sparkle, and for sharing my vision of stories that have to be told. Thank you for your friendship, wisdom and support.

Helen Zegerman Schwimmer, talented writer, editor and dear friend, your uncanny radar picks up nuances resonating from survivors' souls. You chronicle their truths with care and loving accuracy so that they connect with us again. Your important suggestions and further nurturing of my writing, the nagging loose thread that woke you in the middle of the night to be re-woven just right into the text, shows how deeply this work entered your heart. Thank you again and again.

At last, and by no means least, thank you Steve Zucker, dear heart, for your unflagging interest and support of my efforts in bringing this work together. You are a wonderful photographer and a steady companion, eager and willing to listen to a new story or a new angle on an old story, always providing comfort when I cried, making me laugh for balance and perspective. Your encouragement helped me move forward to finish the task.

Thank you to anyone who has been part of this process and whom I haven't mentioned. Forgive me if I forgot you.

Finally, blessings to the 80,000 Jewish souls of Vilna who didn't survive. May they be our emissaries in the world to come.

PART ONE

"There are three crowns. The crown of Torah, the crown of priesthood, and the crown of kingship. But the crown of a good name exceeds them all."

Ethics of the Fathers 4:17

Introduction

These are the stories of my parents, Max Beker and Fania Durmashkin-Beker, musicians and Holocaust survivors. I am proud to say this is my story as well.

Max and Fania were deeply sensitive, loving people, appreciative, hardworking U.S. citizens, talented musicians and humorously ironic about life. They were modest, never called attention to themselves or thought of themselves as extraordinary in any way. They lived upstanding, simple lives, were generous to their friends, family and neighbors, and lived the pain of their memories and losses with dignity, grace, humanity, and quiet pride. Never for a moment did they abandon the burden of their searing Holocaust legacy.

There wasn't one special moment when I remember my parents sitting down to tell me about their lives in Europe. My entire childhood was permeated with stories of their own childhoods, of their family members, of growing up in Vilna, of music, concerts, of life in Vilna for the Jews. It was a culturally rich city for Jews, and so nurtured a community of true Jewish intellectual and artistic growth. But it also had its downsides. Anti-Semitism was inescapable and economic sustenance was always a challenge, especially for musicians like my parents' families.

My father told me that his family was quite poor, but very loving. One day, his mother woke up with a cold and had to stay in bed. He and his brothers and sisters were so distressed by this they walked around whispering all day, worried about her. His father was an oboist. At night, when his father would come home late after a concert performance, he'd run into the house out of breath. He'd been chased by local anti-Semitic hooligans. I asked, "But how did they know he was Jewish?"

My father said, "We just looked different from the Polish population. They always knew."

He also told me that one day he was passing a fancy grocery store and a crowd of people had gathered in front of the window. He went over to look. The grocer had somehow gotten a crate of bananas and was displaying them. Bananas were clearly a novelty in Vilna, and it was the first time my father had seen one.

Then, he remembered that many streets in Vilna were unpaved, and when it rained, the roads turned to mud, so that large planks of wood had to be placed over them to allow pedestrians to walk across.

Throughout my childhood, I remember the painful times when my parents talked about their loved, lost family members, how they'd lived and died. What a burden and a punishment for my parents! I absorbed their pain, wanted to make them happy, and felt how enormous that responsibility was! How could I ever replace all those extraordinary people? How could I even try? My parents never made me feel directly responsible for their happiness, but I felt compelled to be, and inadequate to the task. In fact, my parents were extremely happy with me, but, like them, I could never forget. Their history is my history, coloring my world, often with sadness, but also with richness and keen appreciation. The horrors of the past cannot be made less horrible, but they can be shared. They can touch our hearts and teach us about dignity, respect, tolerance and the endurance of the human spirit.

About 20 years ago, I asked both of them to write down everything they remembered or wanted to say about their lives in

Max Beker.

Fania Durmashkin-Beker.

their hometown, Vilna, Lithuania, and what happened to them during World War II and the Holocaust. And so they did. "Can we write in Yiddish?" they asked. "Of course!" I answered. A few years after that, I was in Israel and visited the Hebrew University library to find information about both their families.

Although I didn't know it then, I had begun writing this book. Like a movie camera, my lens opens with a broad view then zooms in on particulars. Vilna, now Vilnius, Lithuania, had a rich cultural Jewish history long before my parents were born, and they came into the world during a period when Jewish life was flourishing in the city. I needed to provide a context for the texture of their early lives, and so an overview of Vilna's rich Jewish history opens the story. Then, my earliest memories of our lives together set the tone for their personal accounts in their own voices. My parents also left behind a treasure trove of photographs, letters, and documents. These visuals create a story of their own, as well as enhancing the written recollections.

My purpose in setting down these precious memoirs is solely to honor my parents. They truly lived the values they'd learned at home—that life was precious, and family, most precious of all. Because of their deep sense of decency and their giving spirit, because they survived brutality beyond bearing and inspired others with music during dark times, and because they chose to stay out of the limelight, they are heroes.

Currently, a significant number of Holocaust survivor memoirs are being published. Undoubtedly this is because our survivors are slowly leaving us and, just as I'd feared, with their departures, the conscience of the world is dimming. New and bizarre international atrocities and accusations against the Jews fill the news. As a result, there cannot be enough of these memoirs in print or in the electronic media to touch the minds and hearts of everyone who will read and absorb the lessons from the past.

If my parents were alive today, they would caution me not to put them under a spotlight. I'm sorry, my dear ones, but I must. You are my inspiration. Just as you shared the music, created light, and were a source of spiritual resistance for so many others, I must share your story and broaden the beacon's beam. I love and miss you both beyond measure. May your memories and your stories be a blessing upon all of us.

CHAPTER 1
Vilnius: A Short History

Vilna, now known as Vilnius, is the cultural center of Lithuania and the birthplace of my parents. Amazingly, at the turn of the 21st century, it is experiencing a renaissance and has become a major tourist attraction. People from around the world visit its restored twisted cobbled streets, its cafés, and medieval courtyards. Music in the air emanates from concert halls and theaters. Against this backdrop, Jewish secular and religious life is re-emerging, declaring its right to exist once more. A vanguard of concerned individuals at its Jewish Gaon State Museum guards the remnants of Vilna's extraordinary Jewish history. Professors teach this history at Vilna University's Yiddish Institute. And Jewish music is once again being played: in auditoriums, coffee houses, and churches, and at memorial concerts that commemorate Vilna's ghetto songs, its murdered songwriters, composers, conductors, novelists, poets and musicians.

The rich fabric that was Jewish Vilna at the beginning of the 20th century and through World War II has been irreparably torn. The complex weave of cultural and intellectual life, the variety of personalities, predictable inter-organizational feuds, the bonded, loving families, the culture's dedication to modern and ancient traditions–to art, science and religion–the talent that flourished for a moment in time, and that it offered to the world, will never be seen again. Vilna began as a dream that burned brightly and was extinguished brutally.

In the first half of the 14th century, the ruler of the Grand Duchy of Lithuania imagined a great city rising on a hill overlooking the River Vilia. He built the city and fortress with the river running through it. In 1322, Vilna became his capitol city. Duke Gedymin, understanding the benefits of trade, invited merchants and craftsmen from the surrounding areas to live and do business in this new city. There are conflicting historical accounts of a Jewish community in Vilna during that era, but there is no documentary evidence of Jewish life there until the 15th and 16th centuries, when Jews began to settle there in great numbers after the Inquisition expelled them from Spain and then from Portugal.[1]

The fate of Vilna's Jews most often hung on economic barometers. Depending on who ruled and the financial condition of the Duke of the moment, the status of Vilna's Jews varied. They were forced to live in a designated area of the city, a ghetto, where many also worked. When there was economic expansion, the rights of the Jews were expanded. When there was economic contraction, their rights were restricted.[2]

Medieval Vilna had more restrictive laws, while 17th-century Vilna allowed Jews to live outside the designated ghetto. During the first half of the 17th century, wealthy Jewish emigrants and scholars arrived from Prague, Frankfurt, and Polish towns. In 1652, a Kehillah or Kahal (official Jewish governing body and court) was established. In 1800, a sacred shrine was built on the site of the Great Synagogue (Schulhof), where the Vilna Gaon (Eminence), Elijah ben Solomon Zalman, once lived. Jewish pilgrims from all over Europe traveled to worship in it, and in 1812, when Napoleon headquartered in Vilna for eighteen days during his campaign against Russia, he paid a visit. It was a large, imposing stone, iron, and wood structure and legend has it that upon viewing it, Napoleon exclaimed, "This is the Jerusalem of Lithuania!"[3]

In the 1890s, under Russia's oppressive rule, the Jews of Vilna deeply immersed themselves in religious studies. With the Enlightenment, the pursuit of secular scientific subjects— chemistry, physics and anatomy—was no longer anathema, especially since these subjects were discussed in the teachings of the Vilna Gaon, the Talmud, and Moses Maimonides. This led to the birth of the Jewish Enlightenment, the Haskalah movement, founded in 1830, which cultivated Hebrew literature and the advancement of humanism. For the first time, a "new" Hebrew began borrowing words from the Talmud, laying the foundation for modern Hebrew. Religiously, it led to the creation of the Reform movement, but beyond all that, the Haskalah found expression in Yiddish, where it exercised great influence among the Jewish people, who began producing literature in that language. Many Yiddish works were first created in Vilna. Novels of all types, plays, poetry, satires, ballads, and folklore, as well as works of a religious, critical, and educational nature, were written in great quantity. Yiddish writers were born there and others were attracted to the city as its literary reputation grew. One of the most notable writers of the city was Mendele Mocher Seforim, who began writing in 1872.[4]

This burgeoning of Jewish culture coincided with a dramatic increase of the Jewish population in the city. In 1765, when the Vilna Gaon was 45 years old, the Jewish population was 3,887. By 1912, 77, 533 Jews lived there. The May Laws of 1882, which prohibited Jews from living in rural areas, brought a large number of Jews to Vilna as well. Every third inhabitant of the city was Jewish and brought a distinct Jewish flavor to the city.

Amazingly, 98.9 percent of the Jews in the province of Vilna used Yiddish as their everyday language of communication. Although other cities, such as Warsaw, Odessa. and Lodz, had larger Jewish populations, Vilna became the cultural capital of Russian Jewry.[5]

Another factor nurturing the city's growing cultural development was the establishment of Jewish schools. The first Jewish school is believed to have been founded in 1810 by Naphtali Herz Schulman, but was closed by Orthodox opposition. In 1847, the famous Rabbinical Seminary was opened. Directed by Hirsch Katzenellenbogen, who was assisted by scholars Salkind and Samuel Joseph Finn, the school produced many scholars and rabbis, such as Judah Loeb Kantor (1849-1915), who founded and edited the first Hebrew daily, Ha-Yom, and who later became the Crown's Rabbi in Vilna. This establishment later became a Teacher's Institute, the only one in Russia for the training of Jewish teachers, and oversaw four elementary schools for Jewish children, graduating twelve to thirteen students every year. Towards the end of the 19th century there were twenty other elementary schools for Jewish children called "people's schools," with instruction given in Jewish and secular subjects. In 1893, a Zionist school first opened for girls and then, later, one for boys. In both of these, the language of instruction was Hebrew. Other social welfare institutions included a hospital, a home for the needy aged, and a soup kitchen supported by Jews, which provided free meals for about 30,000 people a year—a good portion of them non-Jews and Jewish soldiers serving in the Lithuanian Army, who were stationed in the city.[6]

At the same time this cultural movement flourished, the economic conditions of Vilna's Jews told a very different story. The Jews were involved in the crafts and trades they'd been engaged in under Polish rule. A number of them had their own workshops and factories in the hosiery, leather, boot, tobacco, and paper industries, and they, in turn, employed thousands of Jewish workers. They were also involved in the export of lumber and grain.

Agriculture outside the city employed 4,000 Jews. But, despite this industriousness, Vilna's Jews suffered from acute poverty. It was said that four-fifths of the city's Jewish population didn't know where their next meal was coming from.[7]

Under these conditions, the socialist movement successfully spread its ideology among Vilna's Jewish workers. By 1886, Jewish workers were forming "circles," reading literature from Western

Europe by Robert Owen, LaSalle, and Plekhanov, a few of the socialist thinkers of the day. They wrote and distributed pamphlets and bulletins in Yiddish, organized meetings and planned strikes. Some of the strikes were successful. Out of this activity, the Bund (General Jewish Workers' Union in Poland and Russia) was formed, a union of sixteen committees from all over the Pale of Russia, which published a popular paper, Der Bund, for the workers, and eventually garnered 30,000 members.[8]

Parallel to the growth of socialism and its revolutionary stirrings was the Zionist movement, based on a secular political philosophy that posited the need for a Jewish homeland. After the Dreyfus Case, where a Jewish army officer was falsely accused and convicted of treason and which confirmed the virulent anti-Semitism so prevalent in even "liberal" France, Theodor Herzl developed Zionism as a response to the endemic European anti-Semitism. Based on the biblical promise of a return of the Jewish people to the Holy Land, Zionism fulfilled a natural religious longing that arose at a time of deep oppression.[9]

At around 1870, an early Hebrew writer from the environs of Vilna, David Gordon (1826-86), wrote a series of articles in which he discussed Jewish nationalism in connection with the rebuilding of Palestine. After the pogroms of 1881, his ideas struck a responsive chord among Vilna's Jews. Secular societies such as Ohabe Zion and Hibat Zion were formed to take steps for resettlement. Orthodox rabbis disdained the movement and said that there could not be an established Jewish state without the advent of the Messiah. In fact, many of their successors would blame Herzl for causing the Holocaust.[10]

In 1895, Theodore Herzl published *Der Judenstaat,* and the movement became more active, especially in Vilna. On August 16, 1904, Herzl spent a day in Vilna, and drew crowds of followers who celebrated his visit and heard him speak. In the wake of his visit, when the British proposed the establishment of a Jewish state in East Africa, a majority of Jews were opposed. A meeting of the Zionists of Russia was held in Vilna in 1905 and resolved that the ultimate aim of Zionism was to establish the state where it was originally located, in the ancient land of Palestine.[11]

World War I broke out in August 1914. From then until 1922, Vilna's Jews experienced great suffering. "They became a prey to economic depression, military requisitions, unemployment, famine and disease; thousands of them were subjected to forced labor, imprisonment, plunder and brutal attacks; and physical and material deterioration inevitably engendered a certain degree of social demoralization. All the variegated differences of principle, of religious outlook and sociological doctrine, were now forgotten...."[12]

After a hundred years of Russian rule, German troops entered Vilna on Yom Kippur 1915. Thousands of Jewish refugees sought refuge in Vilna, but food and shelter were unavailable. The Germans allowed some to go to neighboring villages and towns and others to emigrate. They eventually forbade emigration, mandating that business people remain to try to bolster the collapsing economy. Since these business people were forbidden to travel to other towns to buy and sell materials, industry came to a standstill. Brutal, forced military and labor conscriptions were imposed on the Jewish population by the German invaders. Malnourishment, severe cold, and lack of medical care created typhoid and dysentery epidemics, which decimated the population.[13]

The Germans maintained control for the next three years, until November 1918, during which time the Jews, and most of Europe, suffered extreme privation and oppression. Despite all this, they maintained a strong connection to learning and culture. Zionist Hebrew schools, Talmud Torah institutions, and adult learning classes were well attended. In addition, the Jews also kept the arts alive. "Hundreds of concerts were held, partly for the benefit of needy institutions, partly to dissipate the prevailing gloom. Perhaps the most remarkable product of this period was the 'Vilner Truppe,' a theatrical company of gifted players that came into existence in February 1916. It performed Yiddish plays and works of European dramatists in the

Vilna Municipal Theater, and strikingly exemplified Jewish enthusiasm for...dramatic art."[14]

In April 1919, the Polish Army occupied Vilna, resulting in the severe persecution and arrest of hundreds of Jews and the murder of 70 of them. "A commission sent to investigate by Woodrow Wilson under Henry Morgenthau, Sr., in July 1919, determined that 2,000 Jewish homes and stores had been looted."[15]

On February 20, 1921, Vilna and Vilna province were officially incorporated into Poland, much to the disappointment of the Lithuanian government, which had been lobbying to make it part of Lithuania. "The incorporation of the province of Vilna within the Republic thus made the sorely-tried Jews of that district subject to the policy of illegal and unjust discrimination to which all the other Jews were exposed."[16] Thousands of Jews were denied Polish citizenship and declared stateless. Though they were required to perform the services of citizens and abide by Polish laws, they were not permitted to receive their rights under those laws.[17]

"The dominating character of the social conditions was one of want and depression. The policy pursued by the Polish government and the municipality...sufficed to obstruct the material recovery (from WWI) of the Jews. Recovery was prevented even more effectively by the general economic decline which the city experienced during and after the First World War."[18] Because Vilna was now severed from Russia, many former business avenues and industries were closed. Also, poor Poles from neighboring villages and towns began pouring into Vilna hoping to improve their own economic plights.

Because of the favoritism shown toward Vilna's Polish population, Jewish businesses and work opportunities suffered even more. The poorest of the poor Jews lived in the ghetto in slums and damp, dark cellars.[19]

At Passover 1938, 25,000 out of 60,000 Vilna Jews applied for relief. Hundreds were forced to beg in the streets. To aid the people in this economic and social crisis, seventy-two Jewish philanthropic societies in Vilna reached out to the poor and disenfranchised. One was the Jewish Women's Society (Na'amat), founded in 1924 to train girls in needlework and related trades; it maintained a day care center for working mothers, tried to find husbands who had deserted their families, and created opportunities for lectures and social evenings. Merchants and doctors had their respective clubs and students had their academic societies, even among the poorest of the poor. A slow recovery followed, and the Jewish population reached a stable level of 55,000-60,000 Jews between the two World Wars.[20]

In marked contrast to the economic depression was the robust vitality that continued to distinguish the cultural life of the community.... "[T]here was an impressive cultivation of Jewish lore in all its branches, and the publication of books, both creative and critical, on a variety of subjects. The spirit animating this intellectual activity was that of a community which felt itself wholly Jewish. Conflict of opinion existed as to whether Hebrew or Yiddish was the national tongue—the former championed by the Zionists, who conducted a vigorous propaganda in support of the Jewish National Home in Palestine, and the latter by those who believed that the destiny of their people would continue indefinitely in the Diaspora. In no community in Poland, however, was this conflict less acute, and the intelligentsia and the members of all liberal professions—lawyers, doctors, engineers—all spoke Yiddish and had their stationery printed in that language, as well as in Polish. Moreover, both Hebraists and Yiddishists were agreed in safeguarding the national integrity and treasuring the spiritual legacy of Israel. They were both, like all other Jews in the republic, perfectly loyal to the state and ready to make sacrifices in its defense, but, like the Lithuanians and White Russians, they would not give up anything of their ethnic individuality...They regarded themselves as Polish citizens not only of the Jewish faith, but also of the Jewish nationality...."[21]

Despite this harsh economic climate, three Jewish libraries operated in Vilna. YIVO (Yiddish Scientific Institute) was founded in 1924. YIVO was an archive, library, and research facility that housed a vast array of documentation and artifacts taken from all

Vilna, ca. 1930.

walks of European Jewish life in all subjects–science, history, mathematics, art, literature, politics, sociology, education–consisting of more than 40,000 volumes. It also housed meeting and guest rooms for scholarly conferences.[22]

The Strashun Library, founded in 1893, contained 33,134 volumes and the Mefitzei Haskala Library contained 46,234 volumes. The Jewish Historical and Ethnograhical Society was founded in 1919. Clearly, the Jewish population of Vilna, in spite of severe economic setbacks, maintained and valued an active intellectual life, and participated in cultural, political, and philanthropic pursuits.[23]

"The sense of a vibrant Jewish city between the two world wars, which lived in the memories of most Vilnaites, as unique in its richness and vitality, was based on a multitude of cultural and political options, arguing, and competing with each other. There was in Vilna a highly intelligent, alert, and erudite youth, oriented toward culture and ideas. Some of them left to study in Western Europe; others perished in the Soviet Union, in the partisans, and in the Holocaust. There was a 'war of languages' between Yiddish and Hebrew, between traditional Ashkenazi Hebrew and the Zionist Sephardi Hebrew, and between all of them and the language of culture, Polish; and there was an uninterrupted argument between all the political trends. But all those were dialogues conducted on one stage: they hated each other, enriched each other, and yet needed each other."[24]

In the late 1930s Nazi influence increased, and so did anti-Semitism. Jewish businesses began to feel pressured, and Jewish students at Polish universities were forced to sit in special ghetto seats. They preferred, instead, to stand at the back of the classrooms.[25]

"On September 3, 1939, England and France declared war on Germany, and World War II began. It was the first German Blitzkrieg of the war: within a week, the Polish defense crumbled, the legendary Polish cavalry was no match for the German tanks, and Warsaw was surrounded. Pockets of the Polish army fought on for three more weeks, but the government, along with many of the Polish and Jewish political and intellectual leadership, fled abroad."[26]

In the early days of the German occupation, the Nazis humiliated, tortured and killed Jews, eventually creating and forcing them into walled ghettos in the major Polish cities.

In October 1939, the Soviets turned Vilna over to Lithuania, the city was renamed Vilnius, and became Lithuania's capital. Gangs of rioting Poles, encouraged by the Lithuanian police, looted Jewish stores; 200 Jews were injured. At the same time, thousands of refugees, including writers and intellectuals, tried to enter Vilnius. At the height of this period, Vilna had 80,000 Jews out of a population of 200,000.

In June 1940, the Soviet army re-occupied Vilnius, making it the capital of Soviet Lithuania. Political parties were abolished, newspapers were closed, and Jewish schools became Soviet-Yiddish institutions.[27] "All Jewish public and political institutions were closed down and Jewish banks, factories (265 of the city's 370), wholesale establishments, and real estate holdings were nationalized. Shopkeepers and peddlers were heavily taxed and thus forced to liquidate their businesses while artisans were pressured into organizing themselves into cooperatives."[28] Mass arrests were carried out. Thousands were sent to Siberia as political enemies.

On June 21, 1941, the Germans marched into Vilna. It was taken on June 24th. The Jewish population at this time was 57,000.[29]

There are many accounts of testimony by Jewish survivors who came from different countries in Eastern Europe, and from different geographical areas–farmland, shtetlach (villages), and sophisticated cities. Their stories are linked by a common thread. They are all connected by the diabolical Nazi strategy to psychologically undermine, humiliate, and break the Jewish people's will to live so they would be more pliant when led to their Nazi-planned deaths. This strategy encompassed a set of specific steps which was uniformly applied to all Jewish communities regardless of location, and was all the more poignant because Jews, as part of religious law and social interaction, valued life and family above all.

First, the Nazis separated the Jews from other citizens by forcing them to wear armbands identifying them as Jews. Jewish men were immediately pulled off the streets and from their homes for forced labor or execution. Jews were dismissed from their jobs and taken off of food lines. Jews had to obtain their food supplies before 10 a.m. each day.[30]

Next, they imposed curfews on the Jewish population. They sent Brown-shirt brigades, young Nazis in training, to paint slurs on Jewish storefronts and loot Jewish businesses. Jews were prohibited from attending universities and from using public transportation. They were made to walk in the gutters, not on sidewalks. In the case of Vilna, Jewish homes were looted by Germans and Lithuanians. The Nazis also employed local non-Jewish Lithuanian gangs to randomly snatch Jews off the streets and deliver them to Lukiszki Prison, after which they were taken to Ponary, a recreational picnic ground and forest area just outside Vilna, and executed.[31]

This particular kidnapping tactic continued when the Nazis formed Vilna's two ghettos and forced the Jewish population into those areas. "Armed Lithuanians, wearing white stripes on their left arms, volunteered to serve their German masters. They started riots, organized pogroms, robbed and plundered Jewish shops and homes. Once-friendly townspeople took up Jew-baiting. The Germans picked up Jewish men from the streets, took them to wealthy Jewish homes, and ordered them to pack and load expensive furniture, carpets, pianos, silver, and the pictures off the walls to be shipped to Germany."[32]

"...We learned that one morning before dawn, Germans and Lithuanians took 12,000 to 15,000 men, women and children living in our neighborhood from their beds, loaded them onto big trucks, and drove them to (Lukiszki) prison. Their empty homes became the Vilna Ghetto... A few days later, on September 6, 1941, a new law was passed...all Jews must move into the ghetto."[33]

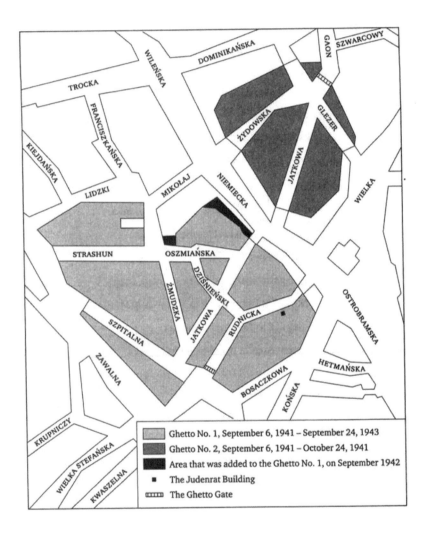

Map of the Vilna Ghetto.
(courtesy of Yad Vashem)

"The creation of the ghetto exposed the cunning nature of the oppressor. In order to unnerve the victims and undermine their possible resolve to resist, all Jews were removed from the comfort of their own homes and resettled in the cramped inhuman ghetto conditions, hardly conducive for normal existence. Initially, there were two ghettos in Vilnius, one on each side of Vokeciu Street...."[34]

The two ghettos consisted of seven narrow streets in what had been a slum and the medieval ghetto area. Vokeciu Street was an important thoroughfare and it was thus kept open to regular city traffic. The large first ghetto, situated in the square between Vokeciu, Arkliu (Konska), Pylimo (Zawalna), and Lydos (Lidska) Streets, was initially occupied by some 29,000 Jews. The smaller second ghetto, composed of Zydu (Zydowska), and Stikliu (Szkliana), Antokolskio (Antokolskego), and Gaono (Gaona) Streets was inhabited by some 11,000 Jews. It also included the courtyard in which the Great Synagogue and many small houses of worship were located.[35]

Creating two ghettos was "a shrewd Nazi ploy. It splintered the Jewish community, broke off lines of communication, and made it easier to carry out the hideous Nazi plans. The second ghetto was doomed from the outset. In October 1941, a number of Nazi actions were conducted with the purpose of reducing the ghetto population. On October 1-2, 1941, on Yom Kippur, the Day of Atonement, 2,200 Jews from the first ghetto and 1,700 from the second, were taken to Ponary for extermination. The following two days another 2,000 Jews were removed from the second ghetto to Ponar. Two weeks later, October 15-16, 1941, 3,000 residents of the second ghetto were transferred to Ponar and murdered the same day. By the last week of October 1941, the second ghetto was virtually empty. For all practical purposes only one ghetto remained in the city. It appeared, however, that the Nazis still entertained some plans for the second ghetto and retained it for a while empty, but intact."[36]

"The ghettos were created by the Nazis with the purpose of dehumanizing, degrading, and oppressing their Jewish inhabitants, and to exploit them as a source of cheap labor in the service of the

German war machine. The Vilna ghetto was not different. It operated on the same principles as did most other ghettos in major East European cities. It was extremely overcrowded. Several unrelated families were usually herded together in one small room. In order to isolate and separate the Jews from their gentile neighbors, walls were erected to cut off the streets that connected the ghetto to the rest of the city. The inhabitants of the ghetto were thus trapped in this large prison camp. To enter or exit from the ghetto was possible only through one gate, continuously guarded from the outside by German soldiers and Lithuanian policemen."[37]

To more effectively control the ghetto population, the Nazis set up a *Jüdenrat*, or a Jewish Council (Jewish governing group consisting of Jews selected by and answering to the Nazis). There were two *Jüdenrats* in the Vilna ghetto. The first had received an impossible, sadistic command from their Nazi overseers: They had to collect three million Reichmarks from the ghetto inhabitants within a very short period of time or they would be executed. Frantically, they appealed to the ghetto population, people who had been torn out of their homes with almost no possessions. The members of the Jüdenrat somehow managed to collect almost the entire amount, short a few thousand Reichmarks, in the allotted time. But because they didn't have the entire sum, they were executed.[38]

The Nazis then selected a new *Jüdenrat* and appointed Yakov Gens as its head, an unenviable position. Gens was viewed by the ghetto population as either a traitor or a savior. He was given Nazi directives to enhance the health, basic well-being, and social activities of the ghetto residents (especially cultural pursuits, sports, and health programs for the children), and requested and received Nazi support for many social welfare and arts programs. He also had to choose who would live or die in Nazi actions. His mandate was to maintain order and quiet in the ghetto, a "business-as-usual" atmosphere, while also knowingly and unknowingly sanctioning mass executions at Ponary and other locations. In making these decisions, he hoped that by sacrificing part of the Jewish community, he would save the majority. Was he a Nazi collaborator or, to the best of his ability, a champion of the Jewish community? There is still no specific answer to this question. His untenable situation came to an end a week before the ghetto was liquidated on September 23, 1943 when the Nazis executed him.[39]

"On July 4, 1941 the Germans ordered a Jüdenrat to be set up. On that same day, the German Einsatzkommando 9 with the assistance of an Ordnungspolizei unit and about 150 Lithuanian police and anti-Soviet 'partisans' commenced mass executions in the Ponary woods about 7 miles from the city. Jews were pulled off the streets and out of their homes and held for a few days at the Lukiszki Prison before being taken to the killing site–big Soviet fuel storage pits surrounded by earthworks. Victims were 'registered,' stripped naked, blindfolded, marched to the edge of the pits, and executed at the rate of 100 per hour. By July 20th, 5,000 Jews had been murdered....Between August 31st and September 3rd, 8,000 men, women and children were murdered at Ponary....On September 6th, the Jews were divided into two ghettoes–30,000 in one and 9,000-11,000 in the other. On that same day, another 6,000 were murdered at Ponary....On September 15th...yet another 2,400 Jews without work permits were seized from the first ghetto and brought to Ponary for execution. On October 1st (Yom Kippur), 1,700 from the second ghetto were taken to the Lukiszki Prison....The second ghetto was liquidated in the course of the month...all murdered in Ponary's 'valley of death'....Roundups and executions continued through November and December. By the end of the year, 34,000 Jews had been murdered."[40]

Under this cloud of horror, ghetto Jews were also hard-pressed not to succumb to starvation and disease. "One of the main concerns of the life of each family in the ghetto was the daily safe return from work of the bread-winner. It was of particular importance because without the food brought in daily by those who worked in the city, many people, in particular those who always stayed within the perimeters of the ghetto, could hardly survive on the meager food rations provided by the Nazi administration. People who had no access to the extra crumbs brought in by relatives who worked outside were doomed to a slow death by malnutrition and starvation. It was, however, forbidden by law to bring anything into the ghetto from the outside. Any attempt to smuggle in some food, or firewood, was regarded as a major crime....It was the task of the Jewish police to check whether Jews returning from work tried to smuggle anything in. Usually, they turned a blind eye to those who tried to bring some food into the ghetto. Occasionally, Lithuanian policemen, standing at the ghetto gates, would search those entering and take away whatever they would find. In some instances, Gestapo officers would arrive unexpectedly and conduct a brutal search of all those returning from work. Their searches were usually ferocious. Everything, including a piece of bread or a few potatoes, was taken away. In order to instill fear in the residents of the ghetto, the so-called 'smugglers' were often beaten, arrested and taken away to the Lukiszka prison. From there they were usually transferred to Ponary for execution."[41]

From early 1942 to the spring of 1943, life in the ghetto was relatively quiet. There was a ghetto hospital, schools, and one hundred active teachers. However, this too was simply a psychological ploy to lull the Jewish population into a misleading feeling of hope.

"Despite the external appearance of a normal life...the ghetto system of government was a devilish invention of the Nazis. It was created with the purpose of deceiving the Jews. By providing those herded together within the ghetto walls with a false sense of security, the Nazis were able to perpetrate and facilitate their next act of mass murder. In fact, the hospital, the home for the aged, and the orphanage were turned, by the occupiers, into gathering stations for all those they regarded as dispensable. From time to time the Gestapo would arrive unexpectedly and remove from the ghetto all the sick, homeless and vulnerable for immediate destruction."[42]

Although daily life was perilous, the imprisoned ghetto Jews were hungry for books. Since they had no access to newspapers or radios, a public library was formed. The ghetto library, located on 6 Strashun Street, opened its doors on September 19, 1941, several days after the ghetto was created. It was always busy and short of books.... "Reading fiction was a means of escaping into another, more beautiful world. After every anti-Jewish action in the ghetto the number of readers would increase… [The Nazis] were also intent on annihilating the Jewish cultural and religious heritage and obliterating everything connected with Jewish intellectual and spiritual life. Since Vilnius was recognized as one of the most important centers of Jewish learning, it received special attention from the Nazi authorities." Under Nazi supervision, "the most important Jewish books from the Strashun and YIVO libraries were sent to Germany, while most other books were sold for pulp, or simply destroyed. Only a fraction of the Jewish books available in Vilnius before the war survived this ravage and only some of the rare books were saved by the few Jews employed by the organization chosen for this task....They risked their lives daily in order to save remnants of the Jewish cultural heritage." [43]

These few Jews, who smuggled as many books and papers as possible into the ghetto in their clothing, were known as The Paper Brigade, and included the poets and writers Abraham Sutzkever and Shmerke Kaczerginski. The ghetto also contained an archive documenting the atrocities of the Nazi occupation, and supported three synagogues as well. [44]

Concert and theater performances were also organized by Jews who had been professionals in the arts before the Nazi takeover. "The ghetto theater was located in the premises of the former so-called small City Hall on 3 Konska (Arkliu) Street. Since Konska Street constituted one of the outside ghetto walls, the only available entrance to the theater was through 6 Rudnicka (Rudninku) Street. The hall contained 315 seats. The theater began its activity early in 1942. During the first year of operation it gave 111 performances and sold 34,804 tickets. The ghetto symphony orchestra, conducted by [my mother's brother] Wolf Durmashkin, as well as Jewish choirs and soloists performed, from time to time, in the same hall." [45]

Wolf Durmashkin.

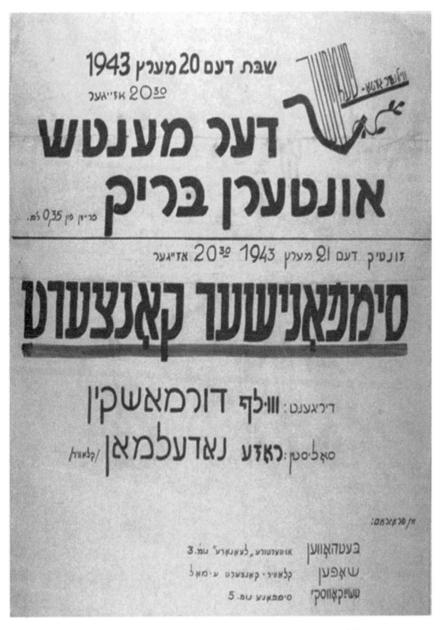

Vilna Ghetto poster featuring Wolf Durmashkin.
(This is one of 280 surviving Vilna Ghetto posters advertising
Jewish cultural, educational and sports events.)
(courtesy of the Lithuanian Central State Archives)

Although many Jewish intellectuals were executed in the early days of the Nazi occupation, those who remained in the ghetto banded together for spiritual and artistic support and formed a union, established on February 5, 1942 at Rudnitsker 17.

Approximately eighty actors, artists, singers, musicians, and dancers joined the union. Among its Board members were Herman Kruk, the library director and chronicler of the Vilna ghetto and labor camp days, and Abraham Sutzkever, the poet. The union commemorated leading artists and writers such as Sholem Aleichem, Mendel Mokher Sforim, and Mark Chagall, and held many lectures and discussions in cooperation with the ghetto theater. Within three months, sixteen events, such as "The Child in Jewish Literature," "Music and Word," and "Baruch Spinoza" were organized. Money was charged for these events and the proceeds given to needy writers and artists, and to families whose breadwinners had been executed.[46]

Following suit, other unions were established in the ghetto, for example, for professional musicians, medical doctors, teachers, scientists, chess players, and the Brit Ivrit (Hebrew Union), which promoted activities in Hebrew, including a Hebrew theater and two Hebrew choruses. The activities of these unions uplifted the morale of the ghetto population, taking their minds off of their dire situations. All of these programs and organizations were supported by Yakov Gens and the *Jüdenrat*. Gens even introduced the concept of competitions to these groups in August 1942. The first was a competition of literary works. In December, a music competition of original work was held which included works by Wulf Beker, my father's uncle. In the same competition, Wolf Durmashkin won an award for his original work, "Elegy of Ponary." Art exhibits were also held, with proceeds going to other charitable causes. Vilna's City Archive houses 280 hand-painted and lettered posters from the Vilna ghetto advertising the profusion of events held over a year and-a-half until its liquidation. Many other posters were destroyed. We can therefore surmise that numerous special events took place in the Vilna ghetto on a daily basis.[47]

Also in the summer of 1942, the Germans ordered groups of the sick and old to be taken to Ponary for execution. In addition, the Germans began to liquidate labor camps in the area as well. Jews fled from the ghetto to the forest and made contact with Soviet partisans. In April 1943, 3,800 Jews were told they were to be taken by the Germans to be reunited with their families. Instead, they were taken to Ponary and executed. Others were sent to concentration camps.[48]

An active Jewish partisan organization (Fareynigte Partizaner Organizatsie (FPO)) in the Vilna Ghetto clandestinely sent people into the forests to fight the Germans. Its original commander was Itsik Vitenberg. When the Gestapo found out about him, they demanded that Yakov Gens give him up or they would destroy the ghetto. Consequently, Gens urged the ghetto inhabitants to surrender Vitenberg, and, in their desperation, the ghetto decided to comply. Vitenberg gave himself up, and committed suicide while in custody. The irony, of course, was that the ghetto was doomed from the outset, despite the sacrifice of Vitenberg. Abba Kovner then became the FPO leader, coining its slogan, "Better to die fighting than to go like sheep to the slaughter." On September 1, 1943, when the Nazis entered the ghetto to liquidate it, the FPO staged an uprising at Shtrashun 12. Ultimately, it failed, but it proved that the Jews were not a people who never fought back.[49]

To avoid another Warsaw Ghetto uprising, the Germans began sending people to labor camps in Estonia. Twenty thousand Jews from Vilna and Kovno were taken to work there for the German war industry. They were brought from Vilna in four different groups at different times. The last group left on September 23-26, 1943, marking the final liquidation of the Vilna Ghetto. Their purpose, according to Hitler's orders, was to build a defense line, an "Eastern Wall" to keep the Russians back.[50]

"On September 18, 1944, Obersturmfuehrer Otto Brenneisen, *Kommandant* of all Estonian camps, arrived in Lagedi (near Klooga), promised to transfer the Jews to a warmer camp, gave them food, and loaded them onto trucks. That was the usual German lie. They were taken to a place forty kilometers from Lagedi, where a big pyre of wooden logs was prepared. The Germans then tied ten to twelve Jews with ropes and ordered them to lie on top of the logs, whereupon they were shot. The others were kept at a distance. The process lasted from 11 a.m. until dark. In the end, the Germans set fire to the pyre. On the 19th, a mass slaughter finished the largest Estonian camp in Klooga. Soon, the Soviet army marched in and found the pyres with the burned bodies."[51] Among them was my uncle, Wolf Durmashkin.

CHAPTER 2
The Durmashkin Family

Music is deeply rooted in the history of the Durmashkin family. As discussed by Cantor Natan Stolnitz[57], my grandfather, Akiva Durmashkin, husband of Sonia (for whom I am named), was born in Mohliv, White Russia. He was the father of my mother, Fania, my aunt, Henia, and my uncle, Wolf, and was a cantor, a writer of cantorial music, a teacher and composer. He was well known in Vilna and all of Eastern Europe, for he had great impact on the musical development of young people and on the entire Jewish community in that region.

Akiva was born in Kiev, and his musical talents were revealed early. He received a scholarship and studied music at the Odessa Conservatory, a great achievement in those days when few Jews had access to most learning institutions. After graduation, he was given a position as director of the Odessa Symphony Orchestra and developed an excellent reputation there.

Akiva's brother, Leo Durmashkin, my mother's uncle, was a painter. He had a wife and daughter, Venya, who became a dancer.

Akiva Durmashkin.

LIETUVOS CENTRINIS VALSTYBĖS ARCHYVAS

Juridinių asmenų registras. Kodas190764187 O.Milašiaus g. 21, LT-10102
Vilnius. Tel. (8 5) 247 7830. Faks. (8 5) 276 5318.
El.p: lcva@archyvai.lt

R.S.Beker   Į 2006-05-31 prašymą
131 Toralemon st.#51
Brooklyn, NY 11201
U.S.A.

PAŽYMA
APIE BEKER IR DURMAŠKIN ŠEIMŲ GYVENIMĄ VILNIAUS MIESTE

2006-06- 0 2   Nr. R4- 2427

Vilniaus miesto magistrato archyviniame fonde, Vilniaus miesto 1930-1939m.

gyventojų registracijos kartotekoje esančioje Durmaškin (Durmaszkin) Kiros registracijos

kortelėje įrašyti: Durmaškin (Durmaszkin) Kira, Volfo (Wolf) ir Ryvos (Rywa)s., g.1881 m., jo

žmona Šeindla (Szejndla), Samzoro ir Esteros d., g.1886 m.; vaikai: Volf (Wolf), g.1914 m.,

Fania, g.1916 m. ir Hendla, g.1920 m., gyvenę Vilniaus mieste, M.Mindaugienės

(buv.Szeptyckiego) g.8 -5 (pavardė, vardai-taip dokumente lenkų kalba).

PAGRINDAS.F.64, ap.28, b.22199

Vilniaus miesto savivaldybės archyviniame fonde, Vilniaus miesto Paupio g.11 namų

knygoje įrašyti: Beker Ber, Bero s., g.1888 m.; Beker (Bekerienė) Ola-Pesia, Izaako, g.1896 m.;

Beker Maks, Bero, g.1916 m.; Beker Srosa, Bero, g.1919 m.; Beker Izrael, , Bero, g.1922 .;

Beker Rocha, Bero, g.1924 m.(vardai, tėvavardžiai-taip dokumente), nuo1935-03-07 apsigyvenę

Paupio g .11, bt.7 ; 1941-09-09 patalpinti į žydų getą.

PAGRINDAS.F.R-643, ap2, b.19851.5a.p.,9a.p., 12a.p.

PASTABA.Daugiau dokumentų apie Durmaškin ir Beker šeimas archyve

saugomuose fonduose nerasta.

Direktorius   Dalius Žižys

Dokumentų naudojimo   Lida Varkauskienė
skyriaus vedėja

Lithuanian Central City Archive, Register of Residents of Vilnius 1930-39. Concerning the Durmashkin family: Durmashkin, Akiva, son of Wolf and Ryva, born 1881; his wife, Shayndl, daughter of Shimshon and Esther, born 1886; and their children, Wolf, born 1914; Fania, born 1916; and Henia, born 1920. They lived in Vilnius at Mindaugines, formerly Shevchenko, 8-5. (Documents are in Polish). In the same registry, found in Vilna in the Paupio 11 book, there are the names Beker, Ber; son of Bero, born 1888; his wife Beker, Olga-Pessiah, daughter of Isaac, born 1896; Beker, Maks, son of Beer, born 1916; Beker, Sonia, daughter of Ber, born 1919; Beker, Israel, son of Ber, born 1922; Beker, Rochel, daughter of Ber, born 1924 (all names are in these documents). From March 7, 1935, they lived at Paupio 11, apt. 7. On September 9, 1941, they went to the Jewish (Vilna) ghetto. There are no more documents concerning the Durmashkin or Beker families in our archives.

Leo Durmashkin and his family. Venya, his daughter,
stands between her parents.

Venya Durmashkin.

Leo had a studio in Vilna, but felt the need to pursue his art in Paris, where he eventually moved to be on his own.

As further related by Cantor Natan Stolnitz, in 1918 Akiva and his family went to Radom, Poland, where he took the position of choir director of the City Synagogue. He established a liturgical choir of a very high standard, which became extremely popular in the city. He composed music to the poetry of a number of Hebrew poets, including C. N. Bialik, taught music to youth groups, and conducted bands, orchestras, and choirs. He also organized a Zionist labor choir of sixty singers and a Zionist labor orchestra, which became important cultural institutions in Radom. In 1919, he established yet another orchestra for the Bund (Jewish Labor Party), and after just ten weeks, the orchestra was at a high enough level to be sought after for special public appearances. A few of these orchestra members eventually immigrated to Israel and became musicians in the Israeli Philharmonic.

In 1920, an event occurred that showcased the impressive musical ability of Akiva Durmashkin and his great inner strength, his commitment to his work, and to the musicians he worked with. One evening, Durmashkin was directing his choir in the biggest hall in the city on the occasion of a Yizkor (memorial) event for the ninety-five martyrs killed in the Lemberg pogrom. The Radom Jews gathered to eulogize and publicly show respect for the victims. Durmashkin had composed texts in Hebrew and Yiddish for the occasion, the choir was singing and the audience was deeply moved. Suddenly, a gunshot rang out. A provocateur had been planted in the hall to fire a gun in order to cause commotion and panic among the listeners. Everyone tried to rush out, and a few people were wounded. But the choir, under Durmashkin's strict command, remained on the stage after he shouted, "Don't lose your composure! No singer should move from his place! We will continue our program out of utmost respect to the martyrs!" And so, they waited anxiously until the police arrived and began imposing order. Then, and only then, did the choir continue the program to its conclusion.[58]

Akiva Durmashkin was also a great lover of Hasidic music and contributed to preserving it as a Jewish cultural treasure. During the First World War, when the Modzhitzer Rebbe, Rabbi Yisroel Taub, also a famous singer and composer of Hasidic songs, lived in Radom, Durmashkin and he became very good friends. Durmashkin wrote many Modzhitzer nigunim (songs) that the Rebbe himself sang for him. In this way, Durmashkin preserved these songs by popularizing them among the greater masses of Jews in general and among Hasidim in particular.[59]

In 1923, two years after my mother was born, Akiva Durmashkin and his family left Radom and moved to Vilna, where Akiva accepted a position to conduct the choir of the Great Synagogue. From 1926 until 1929, Durmashkin worked in the Great Synagogue with the world-famous cantor and tenor, Moshe Koussevitsky, who became the cantor at Vilna's Great Synagogue. He also collaborated with Yossele Rosenblatt, who also sang at the Great Synagogue. My mother remembers these famous men often coming to the Durmashkin home to work with her father, who created musical compositions for them. My grandfather also worked with such cantorial greats as Katzman, Elphand, Sirota, and Rontal.[60]

In July 1938, Akiva Durmashkin went back to Radom and stayed until the High Holidays (Hebrew year 5699). The following year, he was invited to return to the Radom community, where he established a choir of twenty-eight boys and six men and prepared a special repertoire of selected liturgical compositions. He was unable to present the program: World War II broke out and the Nazis were moving on Poland.[61]

Staying until Succoth at the home of the renowned Cantor Rontal of the Radom Synagogue, a distraught Durmashkin, in tears, could think only of how to return to his family in Vilna. Cantor Rontal finally managed to smuggle him back to Vilna (then in Lithuania), endangering his own life in the process.[62]

Akiva's son, my uncle, Wolf Durmashkin, an extraordinarily talented pianist, conductor, and composer, exhibited his musical gifts

Famed cantor Moshe Koussevitsky (2nd row, center)
seated next to Akiva Durmashkin (2nd row, 6th from left).
(From Leyzer Ran, *Jerusalem of Lithuania*,
New York: The Laureate Press, 1974.)

World famous Cantor Yossele Rosenblatt.

Wolf Durmashkin.

Fania Durmashkin, age 15.

as a child. Born in 1914, he displayed his exceptional capabilities at the piano by the age of five. He would listen to the music being played by his father and other musicians in the house and reproduce it by ear on the piano. My grandfather would place a box on the floor in front of the keyboard, and Wolf would stand on it, because he was still too short to reach the keyboard on his own. Then he'd duplicate the music the others had been writing and playing. Everyone in the room would be astonished.

According to Sholom Rosenblum, president of the Radomer Society in Toronto—who sang in Durmashkin's choir and played in his orchestra—the young Wolf showed his musical capabilities when he was only seven years old. Afterward, he participated in his father's rehearsals and performances. After the orchestra played, he was able to advise and demonstrate to each musician how each instrument was played and how its performance could be enhanced. In the presence of his father, he was soon able to direct the choir as well. At the age of eleven, he went on a triumphant concert tour through many cities in Lithuania and Poland.[63]

Initially, Wolf attended a Hebrew gymnasium (high school), and then began attending the Vilna Conservatory of Music. When he completed his studies there, he went to Warsaw to attend the Conservatory of Music, and studied conducting with the great Russian teacher, Valerian Berdiayev.[64]

In 1939, Vilna became part of the Soviet Union and Wolf returned to his family. He became producer, director, and conductor of a Hebrew version of the opera, *Aïda*, which his father helped him arrange. Wolf conducted choirs, bands, and orchestras in the city, and taught music in its high schools. He taught at the Tarbut Hebrew Gymnasium, where his father also taught, and where both men formed and conducted a brass band comprised of students. Wolf's sister, Fania, attended the Yiddish Real Gymnasium and his other sister, Henia, was a student at the Tarbut School. Then Wolf became the conductor of the Vilna Symphony Orchestra.[65]

Hebrew choir under the direction of Wolf Durmashkin.
(From Leyzer Ran, *Jerusalem of Lithuania*
New York: The Laureate Press, 1974.)

Tarbut Hebrew Gymnasium Brass Band, 1927.
Organized by Akiva Durmashkin.
(Courtesy of The Vilna Gaon Jewish State Museum.)

"In June 1941, the Nazis took over Vilna, and forced the Durmashkin family to move into the Vilna Ghetto. Despite perilous Nazi treatment of the Jews, random killings, mass executions and the inhumanly crowded living conditions there, Wolf continued to create music and, in so doing, provided a source of hope and relief to the endangered ghetto souls.

Dr. Mark Dworzecki, ghetto diarist, commented that it was impossible to comprehend and believe that a theater for stage performances could be established in the ghetto. The idea of a ghetto theater was initiated by Yakov Gens in December 1941– when mass extermination was suspended for about eighteen months. He summoned conductor Wolf Durmashkin, ballet teacher Nina Gershteyn, and actor Shabse Bliakher and asked them to organize a concert. His rationale was that this would stimulate the will to live, and also give the people a way to forget, for a while at least, the horrors of their everyday lives. The first reaction to the proposal was one of absolute rejection, in particular from the cultural elite (many of them belonging to the Bund) and from the Orthodox Jews. Still, an initiative developed from a number of creative people, among them the poet Avrom Sutzkever, Shabse Bliakher, and the producer Max Viskind. Their first meetings to organize a concert took place in Shabse Bliakher's tiny room on Strashuner 7."[66]

The diarist, Herman Kruk, was initially opposed to the concert, insulted by the apparent frivolity of such an event when the ghetto population faced death and destruction on a daily basis, and when so many had already been killed. However, the next day after the event, Kruk noted that the concert had been a great success, that the audience had so appreciated it, and that it had given the people joy. "The concerts became a popular social event in the ghetto and an impetus for the development of cultural and social life in a sealed-off community."[67]

The evening of January 18 was opened by Yosef Glazman in the hall of the previous Real Gymnasium on Rudnitsker 6. In solemn words of remembrance, he commemorated the Jewish martyrs. These words and the spiritual atmosphere the actors managed to create did not interfere with the feelings of pain and suffering in the audience: they even brought moments of elation. The concert began in total silence with Chaim Nachman Bialik's verse "S'glust zikh mir veynen" ("I Am Astounded to Tears") perfectly performed by Shabse Bliakher. The poem was followed by parts of the opera 'Mirele Efros' and the prayer 'Eyli, Eyli, lama azavtoni?' ("Oh, God, why did You abandon me?") led by Cantor Yosef Idelson. Then a young player, Sonia Rekhtik, performed Chopin's piano concerto and, at the end full of pathos, came 'Di goldene keyt' ("The Golden Chain") by Y. L. Peretz. Avrom Sutzkever remembered that the singer, Luba Levitska, sang a well-known Jewish folk-song, 'Tsvey taybelekh' ("Two Doves")...The concert had a great impact on the people."[68]

In large measure, Wolf Durmashkin's efforts also elevated his own state of mind and prevented him from falling into absolute depression. He organized a 100-voice choir for which he wrote Hebrew songs. He also put together a symphony orchestra with instruments that were smuggled into the ghetto piece by piece. Performances were attended by the ghetto Jews and by the Nazis themselves, who were astonished at the high level of musicianship and professionalism of the participants and their director. These efforts infused vitality, comfort, and spirit to the tortured inhabitants of that hopeless place. Wolf became much loved, and was the musical pride of the ghetto.[69] During its 15 months of existence, the ghetto orchestra performed 35 chamber and symphonic concerts. The last one took place on August 29, 1943, three and a half weeks before the ghetto was liquidated.

In September 1943, the Nazis began liquidating the larger Vilna Ghetto where the Durmashkin family lived. The family was forced into the street for final selection. Akiva and Sonia Durmashkin were chosen for death, their children for work. Wolf was sent to a work camp in Klooga, Estonia, with other Vilna Jews, including the famed writer and diarist, Herman Kruk. Wolf was given hard labor to do, cutting trees in the forest. One of his fingers was cut off in an accident.

Then, on September 18, 1944, only hours before the Russian army arrived to liberate the camp, the inmates were systematically tied together, ten to twelve at a time, placed on logs and shot. Then, the Germans arranged a pyre of logs and bodies and set fire to it. Very few survived. Wolf Durmashkin was not one of them.

While he lived, my uncle, Wolf Durmashkin, created and brought light through music to so many. Because it was as natural to him as breathing, he had no recourse but to create music and share it, lifting all the sorrowful souls who listened to a level beyond the reach of their Nazi tormentors and murderers. For a short while, the Vilna ghetto Jews went to those concerts and felt some comfort, connection, and a sense of being civilized again, of being home. It is unbearable to imagine his final days, full of physical and psychological pain, separated from his family, wondering about their fate, empty of the hope he'd quietly nurtured within himself to be able to live and create. Tragically, all his compositions have been lost, but his name, his story, and his efforts are still celebrated and recognized in his home city.

The two younger sisters, Fania and Henia, graduated from the Vilna Conservatory and were very well liked for their concert performances and their musicianship in the ghetto's Hebrew choir. They were taken to Germany to a number of concentration and work camps where, despite all the horror they experienced, they maintained their musical identities and, with their talent, restored the morale of their persecuted brothers and sisters who were in such need of hope while under constant threat of death.[70]

CHAPTER 3
Fania Durmashkin: My Mother's Story
In Her Own Words

Vilna Childhood

We were a family of five people, my beautiful mother, Sonia, my father, Akiva, my brother Wolf, my sister, Henia, and me, Fania. I was born in Vilna and we lived there for many years. My father was very well-known and made his living in music. He had directed an orchestra for the Czar, directed choirs, taught music in Jewish and Hebrew schools, and led an orchestra in a Hebrew college. Understandably, he very much wanted to provide his children with musical educations. In the state school, he led a choir for world famous cantors and composed liturgical music for them. They came to our home from all over Poland–Sirota, Rontal, and Elphand– and they commissioned his compositions. Even chazzanim (cantors) from America came, including Yossele Rosenblatt and the Koussevitskys.

Wolf showed his exceptional musical talent by the time he was five years old. Papa gave him his first lessons, and soon he was performing piano concerts in different cities in Poland. We all considered him proudly as "our child." Wolf went on to study at the Vilna Conservatory of Music, and, because his genius was so great, the school refused to charge him tuition. Soon he became famous as a wonderful pianist. When he finished at the Conservatory, he wanted more and went to Warsaw to study conducting with Valerian Berdiayev, a Russian professor. Berdiayev took no payment because he recognized Wolf's talent and amazingly allowed him to conduct professionally after just one semester, a task that normally required two years of study.

Coincidental to the Russian takeover of Vilna, Wolf ended his studies and returned to the family. The first thing he did was produce, direct, and conduct a Hebrew version of the opera Aïda–arranged by Papa–and soon he became famous as the conductor of the Vilna Symphony Orchestra, which he conducted beautifully in the classic manner. When posters printed with his picture announced that he would be conducting, the Vilna Symphony performances would sell out. He was young, handsome, talented, and so dignified in his black tie and tails. I remember, at the conclusion of his performances, how the audience would throw flowers to him. Our family always attended the concerts and would go home in a horse and carriage carrying all the flowers he'd received.

I also played piano, and he and I studied in the same conservatory, though I wasn't as talented. We had two pianos at home and since we both loved to practice, we used to bother each other when we practiced at the same time. Wolf would stuff the cracks in the door to muffle the sound of my piano so I wouldn't disturb him. My sister Henia didn't want to play piano. Her dream was to become a singer.

There was always music in the air at our house. Singers and violinists gathered there to see my brother and to make music with him. The street would be full of people who wanted to hear the music coming from our house. Even our smart and devoted cat,

Fania Durmashkin.

Henia Durmashkin.

Tchun, loved the piano. When I practiced, she'd jump up on it and listen as I played. But when the teacher came to accompany Wolf on the violin, the cat would cry, "Meow, meow" because she couldn't take the sound of the violin.

We were all devoted to one another. Making a living with music wasn't easy in those days and my brother would always help us out. He'd give Mama everything he earned, and Mama would say, "Keep it for yourself, you need it." But he'd say, "When I need it, I'll ask," but he never did. Everyday life was very hard for my mother. It was very difficult to keep the house. I remember my brother always said to her, "You'll see. One day I'll get you a beautiful home with all the conveniences in it, and you'll be like a queen." We were very close to each other, and we were very happy.

Papa was very religious. Understandably, my mother was too. We had a kosher home and it was forbidden to play instruments on *Shabbos* (the Jewish Sabbath) or *Yom Tov* (holidays). But Wolf couldn't conform to this so he went to friends' houses to practice. Religious observance also meant that my brother had to *daven* (pray) in the morning before he went to school, and to study Talmud. To honor my father, he did all of that because that was what Papa wanted. But Wolf often didn't wear his *yarmulke* (*kippah* or skull cap), yet whenever he heard Papa coming down the stairs he'd quickly put it on.

We respected our parents and lived in harmony. My sister studied in the Hebrew gymnasium, the Tarbut School, and I studied in the Yiddish Real Gymnasium. Music was my passion and I would perform in concerts. I belonged to Gordonia, a Zionist youth organization, because we wanted to make aliyah (emigrate) to Israel. Israel was very dear to my brother, who loved the Hebrew language and Hebrew writers, especially C. N. Bialik, whose poetry he put to music. He said a thousand times he wanted to go to Jerusalem to study.

That's how our lives went along, quietly, normally. We did and tried the best we could to be a good family, good Jews, and to be excellent musicians.

Gordonia Zionist Youth Group
(Fania, far left).

Then, in the 1930s, we began to hear news about how Jews in other lands were being driven from their homes. We couldn't believe this could happen to us. We didn't think about it, or even allow it into our thoughts. But, unfortunately, the terrible news was that in Germany, the horror, Hitler, came to power, and he wanted to wipe out all the Jews of the world. As I said, we couldn't believe that they could do this to us. But in 1939 the Lithuanian Army came to Vilna, and then the Soviets came. They took the rich Jews, looted their businesses, stole their money, and sent them to Siberia. When the Russians first came to Vilna, singers still came to my brother for accompaniment. I remember one singer, Karp, who asked him to flee with her to Russia; she told him that this would be a good thing. But Mama didn't want to allow this, as Papa was in Radom at the time. So, Wolf remained with the family.

My brother continued to be very involved with his music. At that time, I performed for the Russian Army and played Schuman's concerto for two pianos with my professor, Kruveh. The Russians stayed in Vilna until the Nazis came in 1941. Then, our bitter, terrible *tsuris* (troubles) began.

On June 21, 1941, the Germans marched into Vilna. It was taken on June 24. The lives of the Jewish population were now imperiled. We had to wear patches with yellow stars on our clothes. We weren't allowed to walk on the sidewalks, just in the gutters.

We heard that the Germans were snatching Jews off the streets and from their houses, bringing them to Lukiszki Prison and sending them to Ponary, a picnic ground and forest area outside the city that was used for recreation by Vilnaites. Initially, we did not know that the Nazis had turned it into a killing field where the Jewish population was being shot and thrown into mass graves.

Where the Nazis sent the Jews, no one knew. The Gestapo was going house-to-house, grabbing young Jewish men for what they claimed was work service, but the men never returned. We were afraid to walk in the streets. My brother was very frightened. He thought that if they knocked on the door, he would use a rope to let himself down from the third floor window into the large garden behind our house and make a run for it. We were afraid they'd shoot him if they saw him, and didn't think it was a good plan. Then, the Nazis made a list of all the professional Jews in Vilna, went to each address, and took them away—we still didn't know where to.

Our fear grew with each minute. We cried continuously. We heard that they were taking children. Then the Nazis began to take Jews from all the different neighborhoods and didn't let them take anything along. That included our family. They screamed at us, "Don't take anything in your hands. Leave everything and go out into the street!" Lamentations were heard everywhere.

Vilna Ghetto

It is impossible to describe our pain. Everything that my parents worked for all their lives was left behind—our possessions, our musical work. With stony hearts, bitter, and sorrowful, we left the house and gathered outside in the street. We also didn't know where they were taking us. As they took us through the Vilna streets, the goyim (non-Jews) stared at us. They took us to a neighborhood where there had once been a lot of Jews. The houses were now empty—the Jews having lived there already taken to Ponary. This was now the ghetto.

I'll never forget that day. When we entered the ghetto, I saw a man who had hanged himself from a telephone pole. That was a warning of the tsuris we would have to go through. It was a horrible experience. [The man was Dr. Gershuni, a well-known 80-year-old Jewish doctor. He committed suicide on Sept. 6, 1941 in the courtyard of Strashun 1. Before he hanged himself, he said, "This is our punishment for not going to Eretz Yisrael !" My mother's family was taken to Strashun 7.[71]]

They took us and put us into a few streets, six families to a small apartment. Each family had a small corner in a room and one kitchen was used by all. It's impossible to write about it. I remember Papa, who was very frum, constantly asking the people not to cook or do anything on Shabbos, so that God would help us. I would say to him, "Papa, don't be aggravated. We're not doing this, but we can't tell others what to do."

The ghetto was surrounded by Nazis who established a *Jüdenrat*, a Jewish council. The overseer was Gens. There was also a Jewish police force in the ghetto. The Vilna Symphony Orchestra asked the Nazi overseers to let my brother out of the ghetto to conduct the orchestra because they couldn't do without him, and they allowed it! A guard took him out of the ghetto, went with him to the orchestra's performance, and brought him back. This was a great privilege for my brother. My brother also took me along several times to write music for him. I had to have special permission for this, but as a result, I could see the outside world for a while.

Nazi guards were always standing by the ghetto gate and searched everyone carefully. A piece of bread was impossible to smuggle in. We found out that there were some places in Vilna where not everyone had gone to the ghetto. They had been sent elsewhere, no one knew where. We learned we were among the lucky ones. There were groups who went out of the ghetto to work, back and forth. Once, I joined such a group while they were going out to work not far from our old house. So, I went to the house where we used to live. Our non-Jewish neighbors got nervous when they saw me and told me about our cat, Tchun. She had stayed behind our door for weeks, meowing and mourning for us. She didn't want to go to anyone else–and that is how she died, waiting for us to come home.

Luba Levitska, an opera singer known as the Songbird of the Ghetto, often worked with my brother. One day, she was caught trying to smuggle a bit of food into the ghetto. (Testimony varies as to whether it was a potato, a handful of peas or rice in her pocket.) The ghetto commandant, Weiss, found it hidden in her clothing. The S.S. took her to Lukiszki Prison and put her in a cell. There, she sat and sang the poignant prayer, "Eyli, Eyli" (God, why have You abandoned me?). Her beautiful voice echoed from her cell window to the streets below. Those walking beneath stopped to listen and weep. She was taken to Ponary, singing this lament as she walked, and continued to sing as she stood at the edge of her grave. Then she was shot.

One time, in 1941, my brother came back from the symphony orchestra and told us that the orchestra musicians wanted to hide him, to prevent him from coming back to the ghetto. They loved him. But he was never able to do this because he was too devoted to his family, and he didn't have the heart to hide himself and leave us behind. We never tried to talk him out of it. My sister and I were still young and we didn't know how to help him.

Little by little, we livened up the ghetto. We brought in music and established a theater. Wolf was the first to start a symphony orchestra and arranged a Hebrew choir. He never lost his love of music, and nothing stopped him, not hunger nor the threat of death. Many Jewish musicians had been executed before we arrived, so he worked very hard with the few musicians who were left to achieve his goal to create, compose, and conduct with a quality symphony orchestra in the ghetto. There weren't enough instruments, but my brother didn't let that stop him. When he went out of the ghetto gates, he smuggled back instruments. This was very difficult to do, very risky, but that was how he got the instruments he needed. The police were watching, but he took chances. Eventually, he found forty-eight musicians and formed the symphony orchestra.

I still remember how hard he worked to organize the Hebrew choir. There wasn't anything to eat, but night and day he played and performed Hebrew songs and put together a Hebrew show. Because of his efforts, a Jewish cultural life was created there, and its spirit spread throughout the ghetto to the highest level. My brother presented concerts with the symphony orchestra and the Hebrew choir. No one, especially the Nazis, could believe that those beautiful, clear sounds came from the ghetto as death lay over our heads. They just couldn't believe it. They came to hear the performances until the end. But it didn't affect them at all; they still brought us the worst *tsuris* (troubles).

Launching and maintaining these musical efforts was extraordinarily difficult. A piano had to be found. A team of musicians assigned to work duty outside the ghetto found one in a deserted house, probably once inhabited by Jews who had been shot in Ponary. In order to smuggle it into the ghetto, the team took the piano apart, hid it piece by piece in their clothing and brought it into the ghetto over a period of time. Then piano specialists reassembled it. That was the same piano I and others used at the concerts we held in the ghetto theater. And that was how my brother and others smuggled instruments in.

The first concert of the symphony orchestra was held on March 15, 1942. The program featured Tchaikovsky's *Fifth Symphony*, Dvorak's *"New World" Symphony*, Beethoven's *Ninth Symphony*, Chopin's "Piano Concerto in E minor" and Mozart's "Overture" from *The Marriage of Figaro*. The Hebrew Choir contained over 100 voices, including my sister Henia's, and its first concert featured Handel's Messiah, "Jerushalaim," Zionist pioneer songs, Hasidic and folk songs, many with lyrics by the poet Chaim Nachman Bialik.

In addition, a drama group had been created. It performed *The Eternal Jew*, a musical drama by D. Pinsky. My brother wrote music for the play and organized chamber music concerts and recitals, in addition to composing music, such as the "Elegy of Ponary," which was awarded a prize for best original musical composition in a contest held in the ghetto.

Life in the ghetto was torturous. One day, we suddenly heard great cries in the street, cries from men and women who were being herded out of the ghetto. The Nazis conducted aktions—arbitrarily rounding people up—especially on Jewish holidays. One day, a girl who escaped from Ponary came running in and told us what the Nazis were doing there. She had the luck to get away with her life and came to the ghetto to warn us. We began crying and screaming. It was too awful to endure. It was horrible what they were doing to our dear people, our dear Jews. It was bitter and dark for us.

Soon, we knew the Nazis were liquidating the ghetto (the smaller Vilna ghetto had been liquidated much earlier, its residents sent to Ponary to be shot). Gens, the leader of the *Jüdenrat*, was killed. When my brother heard this, he sat with his head in his hands and didn't know what to do. I'll never forget it. My brother heard this news and said this was the end. We all became like stones. We didn't know how to save ourselves from the Nazis' murderous hands. They started going door to door, taking us out into the streets, and we couldn't save ourselves until the most horrible moment arrived. This was in 1943.

In the ghetto, the Nazis came in like hungry wolves to devour the innocent lambs. It was indescribable. There was such confusion and chaos; we didn't know one person from the other. We were all ordered out into the street for selection. For a while, we stayed together. I'll never forget, Papa asked me if I had a piece of bread. "I'm so hungry." My heart gave out because I had nothing, no one did. We were taken to Rossa Square, next to a church. There were two rows of Gestapo facing each other for about 200 feet.

I saw from a distance that they took my father immediately. My brother and mother were still with me. My brother put rouge and lipstick on my mother to make her look younger. But when we went through the Gestapo with my mother, they pulled her from his arms to the left, and he went to the right. I was left stunned and screamed, "Mama, Mama!" She looked back at me. The Gestapo hit her to make her keep going. One of them hit me to go to the right. These were the last moments I saw my dear mother, father, and brother. My heart broke with pain. We didn't know what would happen to us, or to them, but it didn't take long for us to find out. The men were sent out separately, the older women went left, and the young women, my sister and I, went to the right. Right was the path to work, left to death. The older men went to wagons with the older women. The young men went to work.

My eyes were swollen with tears day and night. No one in the world tried to help us. The Nazis did what they wanted with us. My life was worth nothing where I didn't have my dear ones. I missed my dear brother Wolf. They took him away somewhere, but we didn't know where. They took us to a gate, and there were two men and a woman hanged on poles. When we saw this, we began to cry and scream. The woman was still alive, and she began to move her head back and forth. She understood why we were lamenting. She was trying to tell us, "No, they won't do this to you." She had done something against the Nazis and that's why she'd been hanged. (They were three partisans: Abrasha Chwojnik, Grisha Kaplan, and Osia Bick, who had been caught coming back into the ghetto through a sewer). Then, they pushed us into cattle trains and we were taken to Riga, Latvia, to a work camp at Kaiserwald. There, I found out that my brother had been taken to Estonia and Klooga. I was always alert to the chance of getting a message to him, but it was impossible.

Captivity in Labor and Concentration Camps

In Riga, we worked outdoors. There were also non-Jews there. They were in a separate place with barbed wire around them. We could talk to them softly when the Nazis weren't there. We were building canals, and carrying bags of cement to be mixed with water. Once, we saw through the barbed wire that a transport of new workers had arrived. I tried to get closer to the barbed wire when the Nazis weren't there and made contact with a few workers on the other side. I found out they had come there from Estonia, where Wolf was supposed to be. They also said that there were a lot of Jewish men there. I wrote a note to my brother and begged one of them to give it to him. I wanted to let him know I was alive.

We were in Riga for a long time. Then my sister and I were sent to Dinawerke, and, after a year, to Stutthoff and, finally, to Dachau.

We were stunned by what we saw there. In front of my eyes, I saw mountains of hands and feet, pieces of bodies of people and children. I couldn't get over it. I was sure that they would kill us. They led us through the camp so we could see what the barbarians had done. We saw the ovens where our loved ones were burned. I saw in the distance a group of Jewish men kneeling on the ground and a woman kapo screaming at them, ordering them around. We had to go past them. To my great wonder, I saw our neighbor from Vilna, a cantor, who often came to my father's house. My father had written different pieces of cantorial music for him. His name was Edelson. We saw each other, but we didn't dare show that we knew each other or the kapo would have done the worst to us. We only looked at each other. It was enough just to know we were alive. (After the liberation, we met again, and we still get together with the Vilner at Nusach Vilne. When I see him, I remember my shtoob (home), my father, my mother, and how I accompanied him on the piano.)

After a while, they brought us to Kovno, and we found out that we were just passing through Dachau. We had been brought there, not for killing, but for work. After a short time, we went to Landsberg, Lager 1, a sub-camp of Dachau. Here, everyone was assigned to specific work. I was given work, but not outdoors. The whole Nazi structure there consisted of officers who lived in small houses. I was the cleaning lady in an officer's house. He was a doctor. I worked in his house all day. A German guard would pick me up and bring me to the doctor's house to work, and bring me back again. The doctor was very good to me. He was always interested in me, my family, my background. I told him I was from a musical family, that my brother was a pianist and so was I. He had a lot of respect for me. He gave me warm clothes in the winter. He told me to eat where the officers ate. Whatever he gave me I shared with my sister and others.

He appreciated the work I did for him. When his friends came to see him, he always told them what good work I did. On one occasion, when a group of officers came to visit, some of them made insulting comments about me, and he admonished them. "She's a pianist," he told them. No one could believe it. I was terribly lucky. He was really good to me. He always told me I did the work for him as if I did it for myself. That was correct. To this day, that's how I do things.

What I do, I must do well. I was truly very lucky. From his house, I'd hear cries and screams from the camp. If any of the officers found as much as a potato skin on a Jew, they'd beat him so badly he'd scream. I was stunned.

One night, they woke me because the doctor's wife and child had arrived at his cottage. The guard brought me to the house and I met them. The doctor's wife was also nice to me, appreciated my work, and complimented me. I did whatever was needed whenever friends came over, and this went on for a long while.

One day, the doctor hinted to me that something bad would soon happen to the Jews in the camp. Understandably, he couldn't say anything directly. A short while later, in the middle of the night, we heard sirens and were ordered to meet in the central part of the camp. No one knew what was happening. We all ran out as ordered.

Liberation

We were herded together and evacuated the camp, marching for days and weeks into the mountains. We had to fend for ourselves along the way. I believe the Nazis knew they were losing the war and were marching us into the mountains to kill us, to throw us off a mountain. It was unbearable. Finally, one day, we realized that the Nazis had run off and left us. We heard the sound of tanks, American tanks! We couldn't believe it! We were finally free!

I was told later that the doctor I'd worked for tried to find me among all the hundreds of people who gathered in the camp before it was evacuated. He rode slowly through the crowds on his motorcycle trying to save me from what he thought would be my death. Of course, he didn't find me. I heard he went back to his little house and, with his wife, took poison and died there after giving their child to someone they knew in the countryside nearby.

Chapter 4
Max Beker: My Father's Story
In His Own Words

Vilna Childhood

My childhood in Vilna was filled with family and Jewish life. My father, Berel, and my mother, Pessieh, had seven children— Leib, Max, Sonia, Yisroel, Rochele, Perele, and the youngest, Noachel. We were very happy, but because my father was a musician, and the musical profession wasn't very well paid, our economic position was not that of the especially well off. There was poverty all over, and where there's poverty, who thinks about music? Since there were more important issues in the country than music, symphony orchestras and other musical organizations weren't subsidized by the government and so musicians had to find work wherever they could.

My father played oboe in the Vilna Symphony Orchestra. My brother, Leib, specialized in percussion instruments, and I studied violin in the Vilna Music Conservatory. Later, I played classical and popular music professionally in revues, cafés, and homes. My father, my brother, and I thus made a living in the music profession, and this is how we supported our family.

With the rise of Nazism and fascism in Europe, life in Poland, while never easy, became more difficult day by day. There were pogroms and Jews were frequently beaten up in the streets. Where once Jews had been permitted entry into universities, now such attendance was greatly diminished as gentile students became increasingly emboldened to "educate" (beat up) Jews they'd look for in the streets. Once, tired of the persistent abuse and assaults, a group of Jewish butchers in Vilna banded together, with cleavers in hand, to offer some "re-education" to their tormentors. One student, a thug who frequently inflamed the pack, learned the fine art of kosher meat cutting that day, never to bother Jews again.

We lived on the same street as my maternal grandparents— Zelda and Yitzchok—my aunts, and my cousins. We were really so close that we never said "aunt," "uncle" or "grandma," instead calling everyone by his or her first name. One of my mother's sisters was named Nachamel, and to us children she was almost like a sister as well.

All of us attended a Jewish school; we never went to a non-Jewish public school. Though we were all educated in Yiddish— at home, in the street, with our families, and grandparents, we always spoke Yiddish—we still had to learn Polish in order to communicate in the Polish world around us. But our whole life was a strictly traditional Jewish one.

We were closer to our mother's side of the family because we were brought up on the same street with all of my mother's relatives. My father's side of the family lived farther away, and relations with them were good but more formal. For instance, if we were punished by our parents—as all parents do occasionally— we used to hide in our grandparents' house or in our aunt's house so that we wouldn't get caught. My mother had two sisters on the same street as well, married with families. Here were two more places to hide! The third place was the best place of all: grandfather and grandmother. There, we had good protection!

Berel (Boris) Beker.

Pessieh and Leibl Beker, 1915.

Berel Beker.

Chiene Beker.

Berel and Pessieh Beker at grave of Chiene Beker,
Berel's mother.
The stone says:
"Here rests our best, beloved mother and grandmother,
Chiene Rivkeh bat Menachem Mendel Beker."
Zaretche Cemetery, Vilna.

Wulf Beker.

(l-r) Yisroel and Noachel Beker with their cousin.

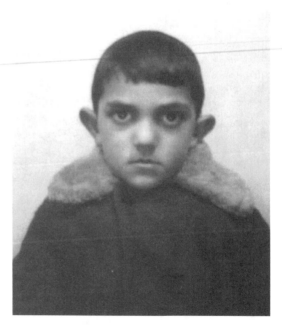

Noachel Beker.

Noachel Beker.

Grisha (George) and Lisa Beker.
As an adult, Lisa married Charles Baker and emigrated
to New York before World War II. She and Charles later
sponsored Max Beker, after the war,
to emigrate to the United States.

Pereleh, Rocheleh, and Yisroel Beker.

Max Beker's family:
(l-r) Boris Beker, Israel Beker, Chiene Beker, Pessieh Beker,
Leibl Beker, his wife Genia, Rocheleh Beker, unknown
woman, Pessieh's sister Nechaml, her husband Abraham,
Max's cousin's wife, Bela, and son, unknown woman; unknown man, Genia's wife's parents; (on floor, l-r) unknown
man, Noachel Beker, Pessieh's sister's son Zelig,
Max's sister Pereleh.

Leibl Beker.

Max Beker, passport photo.

Sonia Beker, Max's sister.

We loved holidays like Passover, Rosh Hashanah, Chanukah, or Purim. The children used to wait especially for Chanukah and Purim because we got *sh'lach mones* (plates filled with sweets and fruits) for Purim and Chanukah gelt (coins) for Chanukah, and that for us as small children was a thrill! Every little thing in the family we used to enjoy very much!

My grandfather, my mother's father, had a cleaning store. Though it was not an easy profession, my grandfather made a living cleaning clothes. Since he was a good man, his reputation helped him earn a comfortable living. All the people in our neighborhood knew Yitzchok der Farber (the dyer of fabrics) and used to bring him their clothes for cleaning.

As one of the many things he did to endear him to the community, a week before Pesach, when all the women had to *kasher* their dishes, pots, and pans and make them kosher for Passover, my grandfather would open to the local womenfolk the vat he used to boil the water to clean clothes. Before he started, a rabbi would come to make sure everything was done according to Jewish law. I remember how he cleaned out the whole vat for them and filled it up with water. Underneath was an oven where he put coal or wood, which he burned to boil the water. And then the women would come with all their utensils. When the water was boiling, he did the kashering for the women. I was my grandfather's helper.

As part of the process, he took a huge basket, put in it all the dishes, pots, and pans individually for each customer and dipped it three times in the water. I remember he used to say, "One, two, three," counting each dip. I used to help him put in the dishes, helped him pick up the basket because it was heavy, and then we'd dip it together. If it was too heavy, he'd divide the items two or three times. For me it was a thrill, because after the week of kashering was over my grandfather gave me some money since I had been his helper. I had a great time!

My family kept a kosher home. We had *fleishig* [meat] dishes and *milchig* [dairy] dishes, and also Pesachdikeh [Passover] dishes which we took out once a year for the holiday. We went to shul every *Shabbos*, and, of course, on holidays–the High Holidays, Rosh Hashanah and Yom Kippur, Passover, and Shavuot. The happiest time was on Pesach when we seven children, my parents, and my grandparents used to sit together at a huge table for the Seder. My mother was a very good cook. We used to sing the Hagaddah (Passover story), and it was really such a happy time, with so many laughs at the table. And when it came to the Afikoman (hidden piece of matzoh), all the children wanted to steal it. It was fun!

Originally from Russia, my father had studied at the St. Petersburg Conservatory of Music. His father had also been educated musically and was an excellent musician as well, having risen to the rank of chief conductor of the Czar's brass band. With a position like that, the family enjoyed a good life. I remember when I was a little boy that we'd visit my father's parents quite often. Grandfather would take out his baton, a gift from the Czar, and show it to me. It was made of ivory with a silver ring around it and was engraved in Russian, "A gift from the Czar."

My father's brother, Wulf, was a very good flute player, and also an excellent musician. Later, when Vilna was part of Poland, he became the chief of the army regiment orchestra. Above him was the captain, the conductor, and it was his duty to prepare the orchestra and all the music for the captain.

My mother was very lovable, beautiful, hardworking, and a good-natured person. She had to take care of seven children and a big apartment. Though the day was too short for her, she was very content and managed very well. She brought love to all the children and to the whole family. We were really a happy family. As we grew older, my parents used to take us all to musical events, like symphony concerts and the opera. As a result, we grew up in a refined environment, reflecting my father's beautiful manners and etiquette. And this is the way all the children were, beautifully behaved, and, like I said before, very close and loving.

Wulf Beker.
In the ghetto, Wulf Beker was a musician and composer who,
at times, collaborated with Wolf Durmashkin. Beker won an
award in December 1942 in a musical competition for original
musical work.[72]

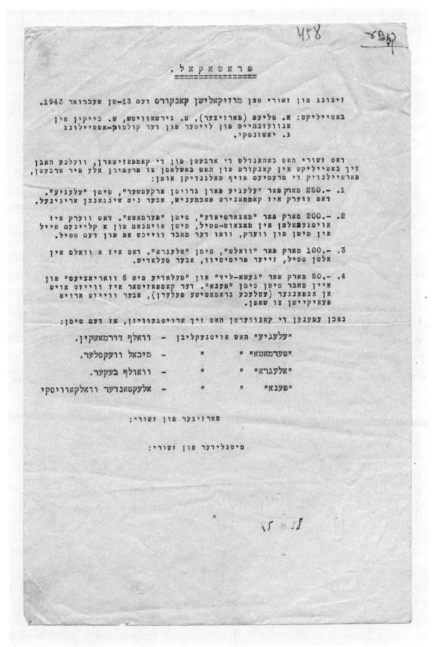

Announcement of prize winners in original musical
composition in the Vilna Ghetto.
Listed are Wolf Durmashkin and Wulf Beker
(courtesy of YIVO).

I joined the Vilna Conservatory of Music and had many friends there. I developed very well musically and participated in many cultural and musical activities. It was a very interesting life for me. I also played professionally because I had to make money to help support my brothers and sisters.

My first job was in a coffee house. We entertained people from six in the evening until eleven. In our town and also throughout Europe, the fashion was that after dinner people went to coffee houses for coffee and pastry. There they would sit and listen to music, both classical and popular. In Vilna, I played in Café Stral, the red one and the green one. (There were three Café Strals—red, green, and white—all very popular.) My brother Leib and I also played in groups with five or six other musicians, as well as in Vilna coffee houses. Occasionally we got a contract—a contract that might last from three months to a year—in nightclubs in different cities or towns. (Such was the life of a musician in Europe.) Over time, I played in a nightclub and had all kinds of different jobs until I finally landed a job in a music hall, similar to Radio City Music Hall. And that was what I did until the war broke out.

In March 1939, I was drafted into the Polish Army. Because I was in the army, the economic situation at home suffered because I couldn't contribute to the household. On September 1st, war broke out when Germany attacked Poland. What had been a difficult life now became a terrible one.

Polish Army

When I first went into the army, we weren't allowed to leave the barracks for six months. Once, I don't remember exactly which month it was, my father came to visit me. We talked about a lot of things, about home, how the children were, how my Mom was, and what was new…a lot of things. But he didn't tell me what the political situation was in the outside world because inside the barracks we weren't supposed to know anything. When we said goodbye, my father cried—and that was new for me because I had never seen my father cry before. There must have been a really good reason for him to cry, I thought, and later I understood that he must have known then we would never see each other again.

On August 28, 1939, they evacuated the whole regiment from the military barracks to a village, a very small place not far from Vilna. We were there about a day and a night. The next morning I suddenly saw my mother in this village and wondered how she got there. I didn't believe it! I thought maybe I was dreaming! I ran over to her and asked, "How come you're here?" and "How did you get here?" She told me that the farmer who sold butter, eggs, and milk in the city had brought her. My mother was a good customer of his. He was from the village where we were stationed and recognized me, though I didn't know him. He then took his horse and wagon, went to the city right away and brought my mother to the village. It was a wonderful thing to see her, but she looked so sorrowful and broken.

The farmer had felt so sorry for her. I almost couldn't bear it. I also couldn't speak too much because the officers were standing around not letting any civilians near the soldiers. But that was how she got the news about me. Those moments, for me and for my mother, were filled with a feeling of togetherness, so full of sentiment. We talked, and I saw she really looked terrible, very aggravated, worried, and distressed, as if she'd been crying. She stayed for about a half-hour because the farmer had to take her back, and then I had to go because we'd received our orders. Before she left, her last words to me were, "Max, write, please. Write a few words wherever you are." And, that's how it was when they evacuated us.

They took us to the trains and we went deep into Poland, near the frontier where the damned Nazis were concentrated, ready to attack. Wherever we were stationed, in little towns or villages, I wrote a few words and I sent them, postcard after postcard. But my family never got them because there was chaos. The war began and I'll never forget those last moments with my mother. Wherever I am and wherever I go, I see her. All my life I remember with pain in my heart that this was the last time I saw my precious mother.

So, on September 1, 1939, they stuffed us, the Polish Army, into transport trains like cattle, and transported us deep into Poland, to Pietkov and Kielce. We were going to fight the Germans, we were going to make war and we were going to win! We were going to smash them! But when we arrived and got out of the trains, the Polish Army was already smashed.

The war with Poland was over. It had been a blitz. The Germans were so well equipped with heavy machinery, and Poland just had little horses and wagons. We didn't know where to run. Sure enough, everybody ran into the woods. In those days, they were firing at us, and at night, the cannon-fire flared and men fell in the hundreds and thousands. As I ran, I felt the bullets whizzing by either side of my head. It was a miracle I wasn't hit. Thank God, I felt strongly that my mother and the Baal Shem, a holy emissary of God, were with me, protecting me.

This is how it went until the middle of September 1939. The Polish Army was beaten and broken, destroyed. Our Polish officers and leaders ran away, carrying their beautiful boots on their shoulders. It was more important for them to save their boots than to save Poland. We fled at night, leaving the heavily wounded laying in the road. Though they begged us to take them with us, I saw a Polish officer cry out in response, "Lay there! I don't know what will become of me!"

We hid in the woods for a week or so. On September 18, the Germans searched the woods. They readily found us and took us prisoner. I don't have to tell you that it was a very hard time. Somehow, I was lucky. It isn't pleasant to tell all the details, but they eventually brought us to Austria and to Stalag 17. That was the first camp we were in. And that was the start of my life as a prisoner of war.

Prisoner-of-War Captivity

First they brought us to the former Polish military barracks in Radom, a big city in Poland. We were there for about two weeks. Then they separated the Jews from the Polish prisoners of war. First, they formed lines, columns, the military way. The German soldiers and the SS were standing guard. While we were standing in columns, we heard the SS yell out, *"Jüden, hieraustretten!"* (Jews, step out!) Of course, a lot of us didn't want to do this because we could imagine what was waiting for us if we did. When we didn't step out, the Polish soldiers, our comrades in arms and also fellow prisoners of war, started to point with their fingers at us and to shout, *"Jüde, Jüde, hier!"* So, we were forced to step up front. The minute we did so, the SS started to beat us with heavy clubs and guns. That's the way our misery started. The Polish non-Jews were put in a barracks while they brought us to the stables where they used to keep the horses. There, we saw what was going on.

There were the civilian Jews of Radom, in the hundreds, maybe in the thousands, with long beards and yarmulkes. Many were being forced to pull wagons with human waste from the latrines, cleaning them with their hands and putting the waste into wagons. Then, they were forced to schlep the wagons like horses. I'm sure they treated their horses better than they treated Jews. Adding to the barbarity of the situation, the SS and the Wehrmacht beat them so that they would run, not walk. The Nazis made them sing Hebrew songs, and stood over them, hitting them with rifles, hollering *"Schnell, schnell!"* ("Fast, fast!") And that was the civilized German race. It was all unbelievable, but it was just the beginning.

From Radom they brought us to Kielce, which was also a big city. And the same thing happened. They put us into the former Polish military barracks, but then the Nazis brought the non-Jewish soldiers into the buildings with beds, showers, and toilets and put us, the Jews, into the stables, where we had to lie on a concrete floor. That happened in October when it was really cold. Besides all we had to take from the Germans, there were also the Polish prisoners of war from Silesia, called the *Volksdeutsche* because their parents or grandparents were Germans.

These *Volksdeutsche* came into the stables and told us to take off our clothes, our jackets and coats, and took them away. We were left just in our undershirts. It was freezing and there was nothing we could do about it. About food, forget it! We didn't have food for weeks, making us so weak and undernourished that when we had to get up off the floor to go outside to the latrine, we had to help each other to get up and then to stay still for a couple of minutes until the dizziness stopped. Then we started to walk, little by little.

The Nazis allowed the Polish Red Cross nurses in Kielce to bring food—sausages, wurst, bread, apples, and coffee—for the non-Jewish prisoners of war. As they made lines for the prisoners to get their food, we, as Polish soldiers, also got on line. The Polish prisoners of war told us to get out of the line. We told them we were also prisoners of war. The Polish soldiers told the Nazis we were Jews, and the Nazis took us out of the line. We had to watch the others fress [eat] while we stood and received nothing—and we had all been in the same army. That was what the Polish army and its soldiers were like.

Although we finally got some clothes to wear, our situation worsened. We realized we had to find a way to get something to eat. So, we sent someone from our group to the barbed wire fence that surrounded the camp. Polish women often came there with food looking for family—sons, husbands—in the camp. But since they couldn't find anyone they knew, they gave us the food. We had to hide this activity from the guards because we weren't allowed to go near the barbed wire.

We were stationed in Kielce for about three weeks. From there, they put us on transport trains, loading us like cattle. Our destination was unknown. For two days, there was no water, no food, nothing! They pushed us along; we never knew whether it was night or day. We had to urinate like animals. Finally, they let us out in a field and herded us together into a large group. It was November or December and very cold. Soon we discovered that we were in Austria, Krems-on-dem-Donau, about 80 miles from Vienna. There, we formed columns and we were marched to a village, Nexendorf, where we saw huge tents. Those were to be our quarters.

This was Stalag 17 in the Nexendorf camp, where we were officially labeled prisoners of war. The Germans began filling out documents for us to send to Geneva, to the International Red Cross. They took our names, the names of our parents, and our personal histories. They asked me what nationality I was. Without hesitation I answered, "I'm Jewish." And they put *"Jüde"* on my documents. That was just pro forma, because officially we had no names in the camp. We just had numbers. My number was 45768.

Then they brought us to a huge tent, housing maybe two or three hundred people. There was no food, no water, and we had to lie on the ground, no boards, just a dirt floor. After a while, a German guard came in and said that he would take us to get some water. About five hundred yards from us, there was a little spigot with running water coming out of the ground. And there, we had to take our military possessions with us to get some water. I don't know how this happened, but I wasn't the first one to get water. I went out a bit later to get some water to drink.

The guard was a huge, fat Austrian. All of a sudden, he asked me where I was going. I said I was going to get some water. He didn't like that and ran over to me. I saw that he wanted to hit me, so I started to run back to the tent. But he was faster and, from behind, he kicked me with his boot in my back. He was big, huge, and powerful. Compared to him I was a little guy, and I was hungry and thirsty. When he kicked me, I fell down and couldn't get up. I had such pain even today I remember it and can still feel how badly it hurt. A few guys from the tent, friends, came out and he told them to pick me up and put me back into the tent. This was one little incident among the tortures I went through in this Nazi "paradise."

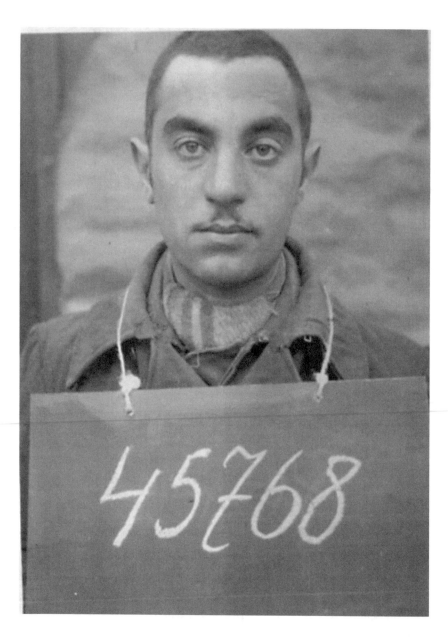

Max Beker, POW.

There were no barracks yet, only tents. The barracks were being built by a German civilian company with a foreman and workers who brought the parts of the barracks to the camp and then put them together. We asked them if they had some work for us or needed extra hands to do the work. So, we worked for them, and we started to talk. They were German, and we talked to them in Yiddish. Somehow, we came to an understanding. They saw our situation. We told them we didn't want money for the work, to just bring bread. "Yes, sure," they said. So, they came everyday, and for each of us they brought bread and a pack of cigarettes, and we were set.

There were separate tents for the Polish soldiers and separate tents for the Jewish soldiers. Wherever we went, whether it was a stalag or tents or barracks, the Jews were always separated in the Jüdenbarracken. We didn't complain because we couldn't do anything about it. The discipline for the Jews was worse than for the others. Anything that wasn't done exactly the way they wanted it done resulted in a beating.

We slept on the naked earth, without winter garments. We endured this because we were young. Soon they put us to work. We built barracks, and then we were called Stalag XVIIB. If we got bread or water, it was frozen. The bread was coarse, made from corn or something like it. The soup was watery. This continued until December. Then the cold became unbearable. We were driven to work, but we had no shoes. The first time they let us into a barrack was Christmas. Then we were finally able to warm up a little.

In the morning they used to bring trucks with "black water" they called coffee. Lunchtime, they brought in military trucks with soup that normally pigs wouldn't even eat, but we didn't have any choice. In the evening, it was the same thing—black water and a slice of bread. We were there until January. And that's the way our life was as prisoners of war in Austria.

In January, they transported us to Mosburg, Bavaria, where we stayed for about a month. There, they built a prison camp, Stalag 7, and we did hard labor under German civilian masters. They drove

Max Beker, Stalag XVIIB dog tag.

us hard, and gave us orders. There was no machinery and we carried everything on our backs. We had to *schlep*, lift, and pull until we finished building the prison camp. The first night we could sleep a little was New Year's Eve. Until then, we didn't have a real night's sleep. The weather was terribly cold and we stayed in tents. Later on, in 1941, they transported us to another camp, not far from Czechoslovakia, Stalag 9, Cieshin. They kept us there for a short time.

In 1942, they pushed us into transport wagons and brought us to Görlitz, a large city near Silesia. There was a big prison camp, Stalag VIIIA. We stayed there for two to three years. In Görlitz, they put us together with more Polish Jewish POWs in a special Jewish barrack. There were bunk beds there, three levels high, and a washroom where you could wash once a week under a shower. In the camp, we made a package of our clothes and they'd collect it and throw it in a space to be deloused, to kill pests. Then, they gave us different clothes. In the morning, they'd give us a slice of bread and a little hot water called coffee. At lunchtime, they gave us watery turnip soup. In the evening they gave us fish that stank up the place. In the same camp, we found thousands of other soldiers–French, Belgian, English and some Polish. Later on, there were Russian prisoners as well. It didn't take long before the Polish soldiers were sent to work. But the Jews were always given the hardest labor.

Initially, the French Jewish prisoners of war were put together with the non-Jewish French prisoners, as were the English. The reason for this was that international commissions, such as the International Red Cross, used to come to inspect the camps and the Germans wanted to show that they were abiding by the Geneva Convention. The inspectors came on and off to check on how the prisoners of war were being treated. Our group, the Polish Jews, didn't have anyone to talk to. All the other national groups had hommes de confiance, men who represented each group to the international commissions. Everyone had a representative, except the Polish Jews.

The French and Belgian soldiers were well taken care of. The Nazis sent them to do different types of work—street building, factories, farming, and other work. But the Jews received the hardest labor: breaking stones, building barracks, etc. When it was necessary to clean the barracks or clean the snow in winter, the Jews did that work.

We were there several months and began to learn about what was going on in the outside world. There were about 500 Jews in the Jewish barrack. In the beginning of 1940, they began bringing Jewish prisoners of war in from different stalags. There was such a concentration of Jews that they started to sort out Jews who, before the war, lived in the new territory the Germans created, the Third Reich that contained Silesia, and so on. They segregated us according to different areas—Poland, Silesia, Pomeron near the ocean—all now parts of the Third Reich. Then, they started to send back the people who came from those territories on transports. Every day, they sent a different group back to Poland. Most were sent to Lublin and Bialipodlask. They wanted to show they were operating according to the Geneva Convention, and were releasing the prisoners of war. Actually, they weren't releasing them. They just sent them back to Poland, to Lublin and Bialipodlask (Belapodlaska), to ghettos and to concentration camps.

They actually took off the POWs' military uniforms and gave them civilian clothes, because as long as these men wore uniforms the Germans couldn't do anything to them. That was the "release," as they called it. They only kept them in the stalag for approximately a year. After that they sent them out every day to ghettos, like Lublin, and concentration camps until the only prisoners left were from Vilna. Vilna at that time was Lithuania, and we were left there from the beginning until the end of 1944.

The real fate of the Jewish prisoners of war sent back to Lublin and Bialipodlask was that the Nazis kept them there in the ghettos for another couple of years. They worked there and they certainly suffered there. But we were told that at the end of 1942 and 1943, the Germans took columns of prisoners at a time into the woods and killed them there, shooting them by the hundreds.

After the war, when I went to Lodz, I met someone who told me all about this, a prisoner of war with whom I had been together in Görlitz. Somehow he got out. He also told me about our leader in captivity, *Kommandant* Dr. Kraut, a Polish prisoner-of-war, a Jew, and a very refined, intelligent man. He was a POW go-between, a *farkoingsman* in Yiddish, in German a *vertraungsman,* a *homme de confiance.* In Poland, he had been a famous lawyer. For all the years in Görlitz he was our leader, treated beautifully by the Germans because they needed him. He'd had better sleeping quarters and better food. But when they finally finished off all the former prisoners of war, they took him out to the woods as well. The *Kommandant,* who'd pretended that he was Kraut's friend, shot him himself. And that was the end of the Jewish prisoners of war in Germany.

Our group in Stalag VIIIA was from Lithuania. Vilna had been given to Lithuania right before the war. The capital had been Kovno, but now since Vilna was part of Lithuania, it became the capital. There were sixty-three Jewish prisoners from Vilna in the camp. They sent us to *Arbeitskommando* (work detail) in Ludwigsdorf, where we had to go about a hundred and twenty feet into the ground to break stones to make cement. Sometimes we went to work on large farms; sometimes we built streets.

For the POWs, life in this stalag was already stabilized. They even had a church with French and Belgian priests. And they had sports in the camp, like soccer. The French and Belgians even established some cultural activities—a library, a theater. Then they formed an orchestra with the music professionals among the Belgian and French prisoners. The conductor was a great musician. There was also a cellist, a great soloist, named Pucell. There was a Frenchman from the famous Trio Pasquier, three brothers from France. We also had professionals from Belgian bands, and from the Paris Symphony Orchestra. Eventually, I joined them. There were

Max (r) and his POW bunkmates playing cards.

Max (center) with fellow POWS.

Enjoying latkes during Chanukah.

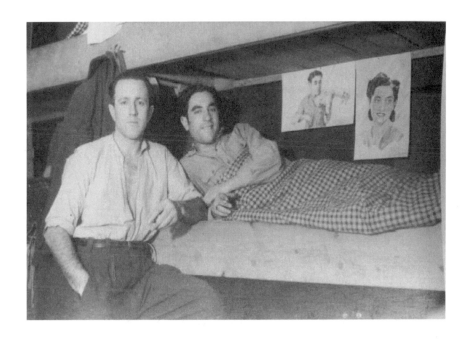

Max and POW bunkmate.
Hanging from his bunk are a pen-and-ink drawing of Max
playing the violin and a watercolor portrait of his sister,
Sonia, done by two fellow POWs.

about 45 musicians, and we could actually call ourselves a small symphony orchestra. We made beautiful music there.

This is how I became a member of the stalag orchestra. One day, as I walked through the camp, I passed some barracks and heard live music being played. When I asked where I was, they told me I was at the Theater Barracks, so I went inside and there was an orchestra rehearsal in progress! The organizers saw that I was a new face and asked me what I wanted. I said I was a Polish prisoner of war and a musician. They asked what I played. I said I was a violinist and someone went to tell the conductor. He came over and introduced himself as Ferdinand Carrion, a Belgian musician. He told me that they'd organized an orchestra with the French and the Belgians, and then he asked me professional questions: Had I performed in Poland and where had I studied music? I told him that in Vilna the musical profession was held in high esteem, that there were two music conservatories—a Polish one and a Jewish one. The Jewish one was called the New Jewish Music Institute, where I studied under its director Raphael Rubinstein, a famous musical expert and opera director who had done *Carmen* in Yiddish. Carrion asked me to come back the next day with my violin to audition.

Where does a prisoner of war get a violin? I had acquired my violin while I was on arbeitscommando. There I had met a very nice man named Otto Hauptman, an Austrian. We had great discussions, and he didn't like what the Germans were doing to us. Hauptman used to come every week or every two weeks, and the boys, knowing I was a musician, asked him if he could get us a violin because I needed a good instrument. We were paid three Marks for our work on arbeitscommando, so all the boys contributed thirty or forty Marks and gave him the money. On his next visit, he brought a violin. It was not a Stradivarius, but it was a violin.

The stalag had an infirmary that provided medical care if someone felt ill. The day after I met Carrion, I said, "I don't feel well," and didn't report to work. I took my violin and auditioned for the conductor. He went to the *Kommandant* of the stalag and said,

Band and orchestra leader Ferdinand Carrion.

"Look, we're a good symphony orchestra, and here we have a good professional violinist. We'd like him to join the orchestra."

Right away, the *Kommandant* said yes—for propaganda purposes. The camp used to present concerts, plays, and theater and brought in some military companies from the German Army to be part of the audience. So, the Germans were able to show international commissions like the International Red Cross that the Germans treated us beautifully, that it was just like home.

After my audition, Carrion asked me to occupy the first violin's seat. On one side were five violinists and on the other side were four.

Once I was in the symphony orchestra, I followed their routine. We rehearsed three times a week and performed two concerts each week. I became very popular and was no longer taken out to work at hard labor. I understood the conductor had arranged this with the head of the camp. The Germans respected Carrion and the orchestra, and I made many friends there. My life was much better than it was before and I got to sleep in a real bed in the infirmary.

All of my other friends were still on *Arbeitskommando*, working hard. I had one especially good friend in that group who used to come to the infirmary when he didn't feel well, and I decided to see how I could help him. The French infirmary doctors liked me and respected me because I was a musician, so I asked them if it would be possible to keep my friend in the infirmary a bit longer because the food was better. Then, aside from the food I got officially, there was plenty of good food available because of the excellent Belgian cooks in the kitchen. Every day they brought me half a loaf of bread, four potatoes, and a piece of horsemeat sausage that was like the best steak today. You had to eat the sausage fast because it could spoil in a half-hour—it turned from red to black that fast! For us it was beautiful because we were much better off than we had been. And that was how it was during the two and-a-half years I was in the orchestra— until the day, at the end of 1944, when the Germans evacuated the stalag because the Russians were advancing.

Stalag VIIIA Symphony Orchestra
(Max is in front in 1st violinist's chair).

The Germans had been interested in having an orchestra because of the laws and regulations of the Geneva Convention. When we formed the orchestra, they took us to Leipzig to buy instruments and choose sheet music. I was the only member of the orchestra from the Polish Army and the only Jew, but Carrion needed me. In Yiddish there's a saying, if there's a thief being hanged and they need someone to steal something, they'll cut the rope. In general, Carrion was very friendly to me and I didn't feel like a prisoner.

The Theater Barracks had a stage, and that's where we performed. We used to make beautiful music, playing symphonies, overtures, and opera pieces. We also formed quartets and trios and played chamber music. We played Mozart, Haydn, and many other composers. We even had a tango orchestra.

The orchestra members respected me very much, and I don't want to brag, but they thought highly enough of me to choose me as the concertmaster. There were also other very good violinists there—six first violins and six second violins. We had alto, bass, cello, trumpets, oboes, and flutes—you name it! We formed a beautiful small symphony orchestra and made good music. It was very interesting passing time like that, and I made many friends.

One morning, we were rehearsing some chamber music. There was a first violin, second violin, and cello. We were on the stage, playing "Eine Kleine Nachtmusik" by Mozart. The stage was lit, but the theater was dark, after all it was just a rehearsal. All of a sudden, we heard, *"Halt!"* and I stopped. I saw a person coming near the stage and recognized him as the camp captain, Captain Hauptman-Lise. We called him The Hanger, such a damned bastard he was. He came close to the stage and asked me, "What are you?" I said, "I'm a prisoner of war." He said, "Yes, but what nationality?" "Oh," I said, "I'm *Jüde.*" He stopped. It was quiet, I should say, for about a couple of minutes. I saw him shaking his head. Then he said to me, *"Weitermachen, weitermachen,"* ("Continue, continue") and turned and walked out.

Stalag VIIIA Brass Band.

Stalag VIIIA Tango Band.

Stalag VIIIA Jazz Band
(Max is to the right holding a saxophone).

Stalag VIIIA Jazz Band.

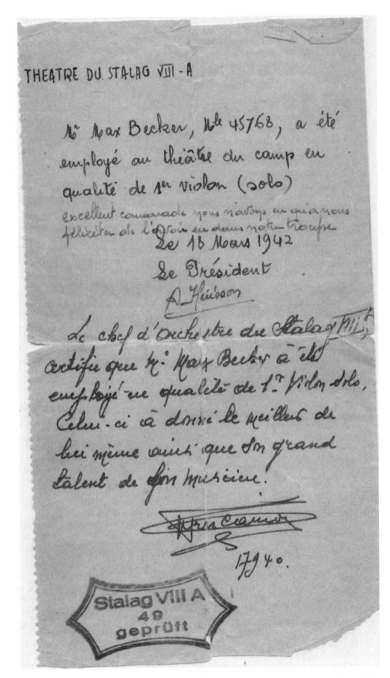

Reference for Max written by Carrion, who states that Max performed with the Stalag VIIIA Orchestra and was an excellent violinist and musician.

Performing at the infirmary.

Attending POW funeral.

Postcard handbill.

Stalag VIIIA Masked Ball.
(Max is standing against the back wall.)

Polish musicians (Max is far left).

Performance for Stalag VIIIA inmates.
(Max is standing left and playing the violin.)

These friendships with the other musicians were very important to me and eased my captivity. When we came to rehearsals, we brought things we could give to each other– cigarettes, food, pieces of soap, or chocolate. We got some of these items from the French and the Belgians, who got them from their families. I didn't have anybody, so I was supported by the International Red Cross. They sent us parcels with food, cigarettes and other items that helped us a lot during our captivity. When we took our fifteen to twenty minute rehearsal breaks, we would share whatever we had received. We really felt we were like a whole family.

There was a violinist in the stalag, a young Belgian fellow about two years younger than I. He was Hubert Paquot from Lieges, a very nice fellow. We became friends. For a very long time he didn't hear from his family or get any packages, and I saw he was always hungry. He didn't have any cigarettes to smoke or any of the other things we managed to get. I was the old-timer there because I had been a prisoner of war since 1939. I offered him some food because I had enough, and cigarettes because he was a big smoker. He accepted, and was very happy and appreciative.

When normal correspondence with his family resumed, they sent him packages. I'm not sure, but the way I understood it he wrote to them and told them he had a friend in the orchestra. He wrote about our friendship to his mother and sister. He probably told them I'd tried to help him a little bit. In a few months, my name was called out. I'd gotten a parcel from Belgium, from his family. They'd sent a package for me! And it was a wonderful package with lots of beautiful things. Over time, I got quite a few packages from them, and my relationship with him was an example of the kinds of relationships we had among the musicians in the orchestra. It gave us a really good feeling.

I wrote a letter back to the Paquot family, to his mother and sister, and thanked them very much for their generosity. In my letters, I tried to show my appreciation and then, little by little, we started a correspondence. I wrote them, they answered me, and it went on

Hubert Paquot (above).
Mother and sister, Gilberte (below).

for quite a while. Then, suddenly I got a letter from them saying that they'd received a warning from the Nazis that they should stop corresponding with Max Beker because I was a Jew and they could get into trouble for that. But they answered me that they didn't care, that I should keep writing. But I had to end it to protect them.

In 1944, I saw something was wrong, something was coming up. One day, Carrion came over to me and told me that they were sending him home and more and more of the French and Belgian prisoners as well. The front was coming closer as the Germans suffered one defeat after another at Russian hands. There were rumors that the camp was going to be evacuated. One day, Carrion came over to say goodbye. The orchestra was disbanded.

A few weeks later, the German camp commander came over to tell us to get ready as the next morning we were to be evacuated for *Arbeitskommando*. The next day transports arrived to take us to Glavitz in Lower-Silesia. From there, they took us nine kilometers to Kipershtetl. A big castle where a prince had lived stood in the middle of the town. They took us into a big building with bunk beds, two levels high, lined with straw. This is where we slept. The next day, they took us to a big yard surrounded by stables that held cows and horses. A German inspector, his family, and some foremen lived in a big house next door. The inspector, a Nazi, came out to the yard with a few of his men. There were about thirty-five Jewish prisoners of war from Vilna, and he divided us into small groups. Each group had its own foreman. Some went to the fields to work on a big farm in Dominium and some to the stables. Some of us were given axes to cut down trees in the forest. As there were no power tools, everything was done by hand. Sometimes, in the winter, we would be on our hands and knees in the snow trying to cut down the trees while the supervisor stood there with a gun and the foreman screamed, "Faster, faster!"

While we worked on the farm, some of us tried to get information about our families. One of us wrote a POW letter—we were allowed to write once a month—to a Polish friend of his whose address he remembered. He wrote to ask about his family, and also asked about

Arbeitskommando on Dominium.

Max on Dominium.

mine. Then he sent it to his friend's address in Vilna. About a month later he got an answer from him that said that all he knew about my family was that nobody was left, that they were all killed in Ponary, a suburb of Vilna where the Nazis killed the Jewish population of Vilna like they killed the Jews in Babi Yar in the Ukraine. My father's brother, the musician Wulf Beker, died of typhus in the Vilna ghetto. I knew then that I didn't have a family anymore.

That was the horrible end of my whole family. My dear mother and my good father gave up their lives for their seven children. My precious mother lived only for her husband and children. Life for us in Vilna had been primitive. The homes were of a low standard. That's why my dearest mother had a hard life, because she had to hold up the family by herself. She never complained. Her family was her source of happiness and satisfaction. My Mameleh arranged everything for us day and night. I cry in my heart for my precious mother, my dearest father, and my sweet brothers and sisters.

Later, in 1944, they took us back to Glavitz, where they put us in transport wagons and brought us back to Görlitz. Back in the stalag, I stood there in sorrow. No more Carrion, no more orchestra, no more music, no more friends. I missed them. But I could not stay lost in my memories for long. We were told to pack up what we had and forced to stand in columns as Germans with bayonets stood guard around us. And then we were ordered to evacuate Stalag VIIIA.

There were thousands of prisoners of war. The Germans formed columns of the French prisoners. They evacuated them on a particular date and took them in one direction. Then they did the same thing with the Belgians, but they did it a couple of days later. These prisoners then headed out in a different direction. Our group was marched for thirteen days without end. When it got dark, they would put us in stables in whatever town was nearby. Understandably, the stalls were empty because the Russians were coming closer and the Germans had stolen the horses. We slept sitting up or lying down. When it got light, they drove us out to start walking again. This death march went on for weeks. We had to find our own food, which was very hard to do. I stayed together with my friend Yossel Pruzan. If he organized [a term used to describe getting food, clothing, etc., by any means available] some food, he'd share it with me, and vice versa.

One early morning, we heard a strange, big noise that got stronger and louder. Then, we saw American warplanes flying over the town near us. All of a sudden, they began strafing the area, shooting at us, not knowing who we were. They must have thought we were German military because we were marching in columns and wearing uniforms. People were killed and wounded right and left. Pruzan and I tried to hide wherever we saw a tree or a rock. The planes flew up and came down again. The situation was awful. We thought we'd never survive this. Suddenly, the planes went away. Yossel looked at me and I looked at him. We both looked at each other and said, "Thank God!" All around us were French and Belgian dead and wounded, all hit by friendly fire.

From that time on, the Germans changed our marching schedule. During the day, they brought us to stables in the villages, and we'd stay there so that nobody could see us. When it got dark, they took us out of the stables and we marched at night. It soon became obvious that we were being marched to nowhere, going in circles, as from one side the Russians were attacking them and advancing, and from the other side the Americans and the English were attacking. This went on until April 15, 1945.

Liberation

On that day, the Germans had brought us to a small farm in Tirendia, Weimar. I thought we should try to get away from the group and told Yossel that we should hide. He agreed. So while the column of prisoners began to march out during the night, we hid in the same stable where we'd been resting during that day. We made a place for ourselves in the hay and waited to hear that the column had left. After they'd gone, we approached the farmer and said we were experienced farm workers and wanted to work for him. He needed workers because the French prisoners of war who had been working for him had gone back to France and he was upset about it. We told him that if he hid us, we'd work for him and gave him a few packs of cigarettes as a bribe. He agreed. He brought us to a big stable filled with hay and told us to sleep there. We stayed in the stable that night. And that's how it was.

German farmers would do anything for a pack of cigarettes, coffee, or chocolate because they didn't have any of that. With the items we had gotten from the American and French Red Cross, we offered something that was not available to them. At this point, what we needed was a little time, so we bought time with our cigarettes and our ersatz coffee–bonenkaffee–that came in jars like Nescafé. Just the smell of it was enough to buy them. And they didn't have any soap, so a piece of soap was valuable. That was how we had to manipulate and maneuver around to get work with the farmer.

That night, we couldn't sleep. We tried to hear what was going on around us. Suddenly, we heard the noise of a car pulling up to the farmer's house. There was knocking at his door. He asked who it was. They said, "SS. Open up because I have a wounded comrade. We have to rest for a couple of hours, and then we'll go on." So, he let them in and then we were really afraid. Maybe he would tell them that we were there. We had taken a chance. But a couple of hours later, we heard the door open and the soldiers climbed back into their vehicle and left.

The second night we slept in the hay. As it began to get light, we heard a new noise, getting louder and louder, nearer and nearer. It sounded like a lot of cars. We didn't want to go out to see, because we were afraid it would be the Germans or SS, so we stayed in the hay. The stall was made of boards especially built for hay, and hay needs air, so the whole stall had big cracks between the boards. If you looked through the cracks, you could see inside and outside.

Liberation.

When the noise got very loud, we looked outside and saw tanks standing there, each one painted with a five-pointed white star. They stopped about 500 yards from where we were hiding. Yossel said they were Russian tanks. I said Russian tanks had red stars. From each tank emerged a man with a helmet we couldn't identify. We tried to hear them speak. We heard the commander giving orders. They weren't speaking German or Russian. They were speaking English! We realized they were Americans.

We came out. The commander saw us and asked, "Who are you?" But we didn't know how to speak English. We didn't understand. So we tried to communicate with our hands, to talk and to explain. He asked us if we could speak German. "Yes, a little." We explained to him that we were Polish prisoners of war and began a brief summary of who we were. While we were standing there talking to the Americans, from the woods someone suddenly started shooting at us, so we fell to the ground right away. The Americans immediately jumped into their tanks and returned fire in the direction of the shots. In a couple of minutes, it was all over. Out of the woods came young boys from the Hitler Youth, in short pants and carrying rifles. At the end of the war Hitler conscripted everybody—old people, young people, boys. Sure enough, the Americans took them away after they confiscated their rifles.

The tank commander, who told us he was a captain, came back and we continued our conversation. He asked me what nationality I was. I said that I was Jewish. "Oh! You're Jewish!" When he heard this, he began speaking to me in broken Yiddish! He said, "Look! I'm Jewish, too! And by the way, do you know what day it is today?" "No," I answered.

"Today is Friday, *Erev Shabbos*. And I remember my mama's gefilte fish! Oh, boy, do I miss it!" And we laughed so much, we became happy! He asked me, "Have you got relatives in America?" "Yes," I said. "I have my father's sister, an aunt, uncle and cousins." He said, "Where do they live?" I said, "They live in Brooklyn." He said, "I live in Brooklyn, too! Do you remember where in Brooklyn they live? Do you remember the address or the street?"

Before the war, I used to write to my aunt in America, so I thought about it and remembered. "259 Snediker Avenue," I told him.

He jumped! He said, "Snediker Avenue?!! I live on Snediker Avenue!!" And he asked me for my name and said, "Look, when I get a chance, I'm going to write a letter to my family about you and this whole incident. And I'll tell them to communicate to your aunt and the family." So, I gave him the names of my aunt and the address. Then we said our goodbyes because he had to continue on his mission.

Later, when I went back to Germany from Poland to be in a DP camp, I wrote to my aunt in America. In her answer, she told me the whole story and gave me the name of the captain. I don't remember it, but I have a photo of him in front of his tank! He kept his word and wrote a letter to his family. They went to see my aunt in person and gave her the message from me. That's when she sent me sponsorship papers and brought me to America. So it was a miraculous coincidence. And that was the story of my liberation!

During our conversation, the tank captain had said to us, "Now, you're free. Now, you can go wherever you think is right for you." The non-Jewish prisoners had no problem. They had countries and cities that would welcome them with open arms; they had families and they knew where they had to go. But for me, after the liberation, I had a big problem. I didn't have anywhere to go. I didn't have a country and I didn't have a family. I was all alone. It took me a couple of days to settle myself and decide what I should do and where I should go.

Some of my French friends from the stalag said to me, "Look. You haven't got anywhere to go, so let's go to France and you'll see what it's like there." So I went to Paris, flown there in a couple of hours by an American transport plane. I was in Paris for only a very short time because life was miserable there. The damned Nazis had taken everything from France. I saw the misery there. Nothing had been established there yet. I went back to Germany.

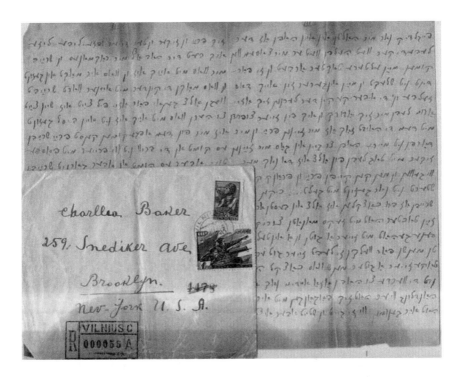

A letter to Brooklyn written by my grandafther, Boris Beker, during the early part of the war shortly before the Beker family was executed at Ponary. (See Appendix)

Meanwhile, the Americans established an American military occupation zone in Germany. They took a barracks that had housed the German army and made temporary camps, not only for the prisoners of war but also for the people from the concentration camps, the survivors. There was a big mish-mosh in Germany right after the war. And that had to be organized somehow, to be established, to give the people food and shelter to sleep until life got normalized.

I went to such a camp, and didn't like it. At that point, there was only one thing on my mind. I had once had such a big family, three brothers and three sisters, parents, uncles, aunts, and cousins. Surely, someone might still be alive. Many were young; maybe somebody had survived. I decided to go back to Poland because I was told that in Lodz there was a large gathering of people from the concentration camps and the ghettos and there I could perhaps really get some news about my family.

It wasn't that easy getting back to Poland, but I managed to get to Lodz. I met quite a few people from my town and asked them if they had any details they could give me about my family. I learned that first the Nazis came to our home, our apartment, and took my father. They told him they were taking him to work but that was a lie because they took all the heads of the families and shot them in Ponary. They said my family was then moved to ghetto number two and number two had been liquidated in a very, very short time. The people in that ghetto had been killed in Ponary. They had been taken to Rudninku 12 and 16 and Strashun 14 in ghetto number two, most of which was liquidated within a couple of months. My uncle, Wulf Beker, remained in the ghetto as a musician and composer. I was told he died there of typhus.[73] They were sure no one from my family was alive.

I stayed in Lodz for over three weeks. One evening, I took a long walk and encountered three Russian officers coming out of a corner bar. They were a little bit drunk and I was still in uniform. They stopped me and asked who I was. I made believe I didn't know what they were talking about, that I didn't understand Russian.

They said to each other, "What are we going to do?" One guy said, "Leave him alone, let him go."

He said, "No, wait! What are you, French?" My hat was a French hat, so I said, "Yes." So, the one who was very drunk said, "Do you have a gun?" And he started to search me. But where did he start to search me? On my wrist! I had a watch and that was the gun he was looking for! He took off my watch and kept it. The other guy, the one guy who said, "Let him go," told him again, "Let him go and leave him alone," and they did. That's how it was in Poland in those days.

While I was in Lodz, there was a terrible incident in the city of Kielce, about 150 miles away. There had been a big pogrom and 41 Jews were killed. These concentration camp survivors, returning to their homes, discovered that their Polish neighbors had taken over their homes and property as soon as the Nazis had taken away the town's Jews. When these Jews came back and wanted their homes again, they were killed.

I realized there was no reason for me to stay in Poland anymore. I prepared to go back to Germany because there was a system of camps already established for displaced persons (DPs) by the Americans in the American zone. From there, with help from organizations like HIAS, the Joint Distribution Committee, and UNRRA, people could emigrate wherever they wanted to. And that's what I did. I went back to Germany. None of this was very simple– I'm giving you a sketch of the situation I was in, and what I had to do and did.

Back in Germany I knew I had to start building my life again. Someone told me there was an orchestra in a DP camp in St. Ottilien, Bavaria, that the orchestra members were from Lithuania, and that there were also musicians from Vilna. I say this all briefly, because it is very hard to remember all the details, and it would take too long. It's already been 45 or 46 years. That's a long time to remember all the details.

I don't actually know how I survived. It was probably a miracle that 63 Jewish soldiers from Lithuania survived at all. Thousands upon thousands of Jewish prisoners of war were sent to Poland, where the Nazis slaughtered them. Only 63 of us survived. We can't understand how or why. How could we go on? We were young, and even in those conditions we had hope. The Jewish people, no matter in what circumstances we are in, always live and hope.

You see, I was there and I know. I went through all this. To this day, I still ask the question, "Why?" Why did they let us live? Why didn't they do anything to us? Of the 61,000 Jewish Polish POWs, only 63 guys from Vilna survived. We were like a drop in the ocean. Someone among the Germans must have made a mistake. But who knows? Maybe they wanted to show the world that they let Jews live, that we'd be the examples. "Here, here are the people! We didn't touch them." Who knows?

What I saw and what I know is that if the American government would have asked me, they might not have helped the Germans the way they did, for example, with the Marshall Plan. The world, including America, and I'm not afraid and don't feel guilty if I say so, stood by and did nothing [or very little]. They knew what was happening. America knows everything about what's going on in the world. With spy organizations and other government organizations, Roosevelt knew everything that was happening.

All my life I've lived with what the Nazis did to my family. I go to sleep with it and I wake up with it. I see them as they really existed. It's a terrible tragedy. No one in the civilized world ever thought about how and why or what was done to us because nobody cared, and nobody cares now. But the victims will never forget. We will never forget and we will live with it always.

Chapter 5
Fania, Max and the St. Ottilien Jewish Orchestra

Both my mother's and father's personal recollections end with the end of the war. But for the survivors, the Holocaust was not over. The DP experience, fraught with its own dangers, lay ahead.

The landscape is tranquil and green with meadows and fruit trees. Birds sing in the background, and circle a charming, old brick church with a graceful spire. The brick is dark with time, but the surrounding buildings are tastefully restored and painted a pale yellow. This is St. Ottilien, a Benedictine monastery founded in 1887, located in Bavaria, Germany, near Munich, near Landsberg, near Dachau.

On St. Ottilien's grounds there is a set of metal gates that marks the entrance to a special space. The gates are of wrought iron and display Stars of David. On the other side is a small, Jewish cemetery. Buried there are Jewish DPs who arrived after the liberation of the concentration camps in 1945, but who were too sick and too starved to survive any further. Some of the gravestones have only first or last names, and no dates of birth, only dates of death. Because it had a hospital building that was used by the Nazis during the war, St. Ottilien became one of the many DP camps established in Germany as a sanitarium and waiting station for many Jewish DPs.

At the end of the war, about 200,000 Jewish DPs, mainly survivors of the concentration camps, presented a special challenge to the American military government. Germany was divided into military occupation zones, and in the American zone, a broad range of new policies were being implemented– the denazification and demilitarization of Germany, its economic rehabilitation, and attempts to halt the spread of communism. The Jews required special attention and the American military was unprepared to give it.[74]

Unlike other DPs, the Jews had no homes to return to. Their families had been slaughtered and their homes and property had been confiscated by the Nazis or looted and stolen by the hostile, local non-Jewish populations of their respective towns and villages. Many towns and villages no longer existed. As a result of Hitler's carefully-implemented plan to annihilate the Jewish people, the survivors had suffered psychological damage, and, to make matters worse, the American War Department urged the military government not to single out the Jews for special treatment; not to disturb the status quo.[75]

The American military felt that repatriation would be the best solution for the Jewish survivors, while the majority of East European Jews understandably feared this solution. It was left to about thirty American Jewish chaplains who passed through Germany during the initial American occupation from April to June 1945 to deal with problems of the Jewish DPs. One of them was Rabbi Abraham Klausner, a Reform rabbi, who did everything he could to make the army understand the unique condition of the Jews. He worked to improve immediate problems–food, clothing, and medicine–and he also made efforts to have Jewish survivors recognized as a separate nationality, establish separate DP camps for them, and create an organization to represent their interests to the military. In addition, he tried to alert American Jews to their situation.[76]

When Klausner arrived in Dachau during the third week of May 1945, conditions there were horrifying. Medical staff members were working continuously to save survivors who could still be saved. Many could not. Klausner officiated over burials and signed death certificates. The Jews who remained alive, however, were not angry or bitter towards him or American Jews for not saving them. Instead, they were eager to join their families and rebuild their lives. Ironically, these Jews were still dressed in their striped camp uniforms and were still forced to live behind barbed wire. Klausner realized that the most important task he could set for himself would be to create a plan to help Jews reunite with their families.[77]

Through contact with other American clergy, he compiled and published volumes listing names of survivors and distributed them throughout the world. In these volumes he also informed the Jewish DPs of their rights, and informed them that they did not have to return to the countries of their origin, that they were able to determine, on their own and without duress, whether they truly wanted to return or emigrate elsewhere.[78]

At the end of the war, survivors liberated from concentration camps were allowed to enter any of the DP camps established by the American army. But Klausner had learned from experience in other DP camps that Jewish survivors often needed protection from harassment and mistreatment by non-Jewish inmates. To remedy this problem, Klausner became involved in placing Jewish DPs in Bavaria in separate Jewish camps. In addition, Jewish survivors were being treated in German hospitals by German doctors, a condition that often traumatized them even further–the Nazis had been their murderers and tormentors and had also performed medical experiments on them in the concentration camps. Klausner thus began a program placing those who needed medical care in hospitals catering especially to Jews.[79]

At many of the DP camps, conditions were inadequate to meet the needs of the inmates. As a result, a rampant black market came into being. As military police were ordered not to allow unofficial supplies to get into the camps, food was smuggled in by conscientious and sometimes by more entrepreneurial American soldiers. Sometimes, women were compelled to trade sex with soldiers for food and clothing. And so, even after the liberation, conditions persisted that permitted thousands of survivors to die from malnutrition and lack of medicine at the hands of their liberators.[80]

St. Ottilien became the first place Klausner brought Jewish DPs. Located in the village of Schwabenhausen, about 30 miles from Munich, the Nazis used St. Otillien as a military hospital during the war. It was still functioning as a hospital in 1945 when Klausner discovered it. Four hundred Jews, mainly former inmates of Dachau, were patients there. He also discovered Dr. Zalman Grinberg, a young physician from Kovno, who was in charge of the hospital.[81]

Dr. Grinberg had himself been a Dachau inmate, and one of the few physicians to survive the concentration camps. At the end of April 1945, word of German defeat and the approaching American troops had spread. A group of approximately 1,200 inmates were herded together by the Germans in charge and told they were going to be transferred to the International Red Cross. They were made to stand for hours, waiting for train transport, when word got out that they were actually being taken to the Tyrol to be executed. Suddenly, American planes swooped down on them, mistakenly strafing the group along with their guards. Everyone broke and ran. Many were killed. The survivors hid in the surrounding forest. Upon determining that the SS guards had actually fled the camp, Dr. Grinberg organized the then 800 skeletal, sick, and starving Dachau survivors, and led them on a trek to find food and medical care. They were careful to remain hidden, as Grinberg knew that German civilians and deserting German soldiers would probably kill them if they were seen. Their progress was slow and painful, but they helped each other inch forward. Many died along the way. At every town, Grinberg begged for assistance and food, but was mocked and turned down. Even American troops they encountered claimed they wanted to help but could only smuggle a few pounds of potatoes and loaves of bread to the survivors.[82]

Finally, Dr. Grinberg and 420 survivors arrived at the church and monastery of St. Ottilien, eighteen miles west of Landsberg. Besides the church, four of the buildings were barely occupied. Grinberg met a Captain Otto B. Raymond from an infantry division a few miles away. Raymond agreed to help Grinberg pose as a representative of the International Red Cross. They went to the commandant of the German hospital at St. Ottilien, and requested permission to bring the survivors to the unoccupied buildings. The commandant refused, stating that the German officers there were too ill to be moved. Raymond and Grinberg knew that was untrue and threatened the commandant with an investigation of the entire complex. Only then did they receive the permission they so urgently required.[83]

Raymond and Grinberg arranged for the wounded survivors to be driven by ambulance to St. Ottilien. Rabbi Klausner moved the German soldiers out and made St. Ottilien a DP hospital strictly for Jewish survivors. They arrived there two weeks after V-E Day. Through Klausner's efforts, other Jewish DP camps were created in Feldafing, previously a training school for Hitler youth, in Landsberg, and at a tuberculosis sanitorium at Gauting, southwest of Munich. Dachau eventually became a processing center for captured Nazis.[84]

On May 27, 1945, Robert L. Hilliard, an American soldier and army newspaper editor in Bavaria, attended a concert being given by and for concentration camp survivors at St. Ottilien. It was called a "liberation concert" to commemorate the survivors' liberation that took place only a month earlier. He thought the concert would make a good story.[85]

"At the far end of the lawn was a stage several feet off the ground, made of nondescript, non-matching wooden boards and covered with a loosely stretched canopy of patched and sewn sheets and discarded parachute cloth. Rows of wooden chairs were set in front of the stage. In the aisles, on the chairs and on the grass, standing, sitting, walking, leaning, lying, were hundreds of stick figures, emaciated, pale, skeletal, expressionless, all dressed in the black and white striped uniforms of the concentration camps. They barely moved, and when they did, it was in the flickering slow motion of early silent films.... Off to the side, I saw other people. In an area separated from the survivors' quarters were dozens of men wearing the green-gray military uniforms of the German armed forces, walking about in the careless manner of the privileged, smoking cigarettes, some with bandaged limbs, some leaning on white-uniformed female nurses, the hands and arms of enlisted men shooting out and up in prompt salutes to the German officers and doctors who passed by....It too looked like a slow-motion film, orchestrated for its sharp, precise, rhythmic movements....Between these two scenes of victim and victimizer...where the winner was the loser and the loser the winner...some of the Germans were able to look directly at the concentration camp survivors.

But there was no indication on their faces that they saw them. Occupying the four buildings on this side of the wall were barely four hundred survivors. It had been only a month since they had been freed, following thirteen years of terror including the past six years of torture. They were without food, without clothing, without medical aid. Four hundred of them in the midst of their former captors and torturers who pretended as though they didn't exist. Four hundred of them, the remnants of millions. Four hundred of them, sick, starving, ragged, dying, on this late spring day in Bavaria, on this afternoon of May 27, 1945. And what were they doing? They were giving a concert!

Onto the stage men and women carried fiddles, horns, bass viols. Through the years in the camps, wood, string, metal parts of instruments had been smuggled, cared for and put together to create music, a link with what they remembered of a rational civilization....Now it was an announcement of their survival. One of the musicians walked slowly to the front of the stage. "This is our liberation concert," he said...A liberation concert at which most of the liberated people were too weak to stand. A liberation concert at which most of the people still could not believe they were free....The

DP camp orchestra.

DP Orchestra.

musicians played Mahler, Mendelssohn and others whose music had been forbidden [by the Nazis] for years. A concert of life and a concert of death. The sounds of the music welled into anguish. The movements and faces of the musicians were cramped, tight, fearful, as if they could not believe there was room to move a bow or air in which to blow a note, as if they momentarily expected guns and clubs to tear apart what, after so many years, must have felt to them only a dream.

"When the concert ended many people were crying, few more openly than I."[86]

The musicians Robert Hilliard was listening to became the "St. Ottilien Jewish Orchestra," later called the "Ex-Concentration Camp Orchestra" and finally named the "Shearith HaPleitah Orchestra," meaning, in Hebrew, the surviving remnant, a term used by Jewish survivors of the Nazi Holocaust to refer to themselves and the communities they formed following the liberation. They were conducted by Michael Hofmekler of the Kovno Ghetto and a former concentration camp inmate. This was the orchestra where my father, Max Beker, was a violinist, my mother, Fania Durmashkin-Beker, was a pianist, and my aunt, Henia Durmashkin-Gurko, was a vocalist.

In April 1945, my mother, Fania, and her sister, Henia, were on a death march from Landsberg, probably to face a fate similar to that planned for the Dachau inmates and the march my father was on. At one point, Henia began veering off the road from exhaustion. My mother, looking out for her, called her name sharply and got her attention in time, thereby saving her life, as the SS shot all those who were too tired or weak to march. Eventually, American tanks intercepted them on the road and their German guards ran away. The inmates were finally free. Eager to begin new lives, to express spiritual triumph through their musical talents, survivor musicians like my mother and her sister began gathering at St. Ottilien. They were starved, weak and ill, requiring care at the hospital. Above all, they required food. Even in a "safe" environment, many were dying daily of starvation.

St. Ottilien Jewish Orchestra

Ex-Concentration Camp Orchestra.

Michael Hofmekler, conductor.

When my father had returned from hunting for his family in Lodz, he looked for a DP camp where he could arrange for emigration. He'd heard about the St. Ottilien Jewish Orchestra, arrived there and became a violinist. He assisted the manager, Jascha Gurewitz, in obtaining extra food, organizing the musicians, and settling disagreements. "If not for Max, there would not have been an orchestra," Jascha claimed. Here my father met my mother, who, with her sister, had preceded him there. As a musician from Vilna, my father knew of the Durmashkin family, especially Wolf, as my grandfather, Berel, had played oboe in the Vilna Symphony Orchestra, and my father's uncle, Wulf Beker, worked with Wolf Durmashkin on musical programs in the Vilna Ghetto. My parents began a courtship, and were soon very much in love.

After the liberation concert, Robert Hilliard and his friend, fellow-soldier Edward Herman, who were greatly moved by the plight of the musicians and Jewish DPs, undertook a campaign to get them food and medicine. At first, they rallied fellow-soldiers to get food from the mess hall for the DPs. Then, after months went by without effective assistance from relief organizations, the two GIs composed, printed and sent out a nine-page letter to hundreds of individuals and Jewish and humanitarian groups throughout the U.S. to let them know of the plight of the DPs at St. Ottilien, and asking for aid. This letter-writing campaign placed Hilliard and Herman in jeopardy, as it was against army regulations to seek such assistance from specific individuals. To get around this, the two soldiers used the salutation, "Dear Friends."[87]

News of their efforts eventually reached President Truman and General Eisenhower, who began investigating their claims. Still, the two GIs persisted in sending more and more letters. Several months later, hundreds of packages, which had been held up in American ports until the origin of the request had been determined, began arriving. The packages were brought in trucks and distributed directly to the DPs.[88]

Meanwhile, the St. Ottilien Jewish Orchestra performed for the American troops, for the patients in sanitariums, and for inmates of

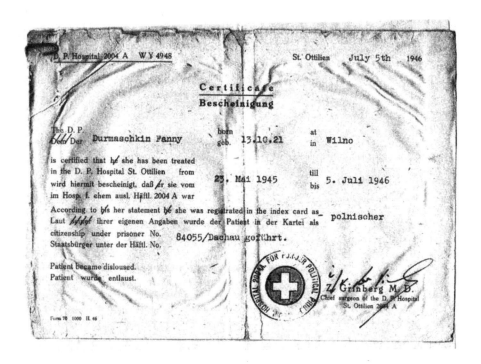

St. Ottilien Hospital Certificate for my mother, Fania Durmashkin-Beker, signed by Dr. Z. Grinberg, 1946.

other DP camps throughout Bavaria. Employed by the Joint Distribution Committee, they toured by bus through Munich, Frankfurt, and Nuremburg, where they performed in the Nuremburg Opera House for the International Tribunal during the Nazi trials. They wore striped concentration camp uniforms at their performances, which displayed a banner proclaiming Am Yisroel Chai–the people of Israel live. They also played for Ben-Gurion and Golda Meir, who came as representatives of Israel, during a visit to St. Ottilien, and at the First Zionist Congress. They gained fame and popularity, and played an important cultural role in restoring Jewish identity postwar, lifting the spirits of all their audiences.[89]

After a year, the orchestra moved to Fürstenfeldbruck, where they became the Ex-Concentration Camp Orchestra. In 1948, Leonard Bernstein was sent to Germany as a cultural liaison to conduct the Munich Symphony Orchestra. When he arrived in Germany, he approached the Jewish Agency and, based on his personal interest, asked if there were any concentration camp survivors who were musicians whom he could contact. He approached the Ex-Concentration Camp Orchestra and asked to work with them as well. After organizing a rehearsal and concert schedule, he conducted the group for two performances. The program contained the overture from the opera *Freischutz* by Carl Maria von Weber, the minuet *Farandol* from the *Suite L'Arlesienne* by Bizet, and Gershwin's *Rhapsody in Blue*, with Bernstein playing the piano and conducting.[90] As a tribute, the orchestra presented him with a concentration camp uniform.[91]

The St. Ottilien Jewish Orchestra played a very special role in post-war DP camp life. During the war, Jews had undergone horrific treatment by the Nazis. Once the war was over, the Jewish survivors found themselves in DP camps where, for the first time since the destruction, they were able to feel secure enough to take stock of what had actually happened to them. The need for spiritual resistance was just as urgent as it was during the war, if not more so, as the

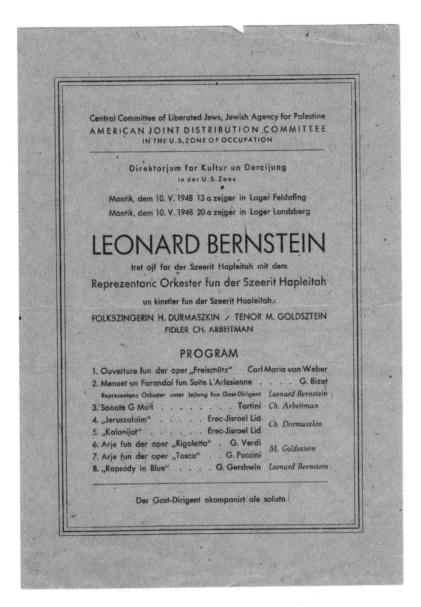

Concert program for Bernstein performances.

Orchestra members with Leonard Bernstein (far right).
Fania Durmashkin-Beker is to his left; Max Beker is fourth
from right; and Henia Durmashkin-Gurko
is seventh from right.

reality of their losses hit them. The St. Ottilien Jewish Orchestra provided survivors with that spiritual resistance and connected them to their lost homes and loved ones. The orchestra performed classical symphonies and Jewish ghetto, folk and Zionist Hebrew songs to grief-eroded souls. It gave them a reason to go on. It said, "Look, we are still here after all that's happened. We can still create something beautiful that we can share with one another and with the world, even though the world didn't care."

In the ghettos and concentration camps, these Jews combined their innate talent, education, and a rich heritage provided by musicians, composers, artists, doctors, philosophers, writers, educators, prophets, and religious figures who had preceded them, and created works of art so brilliant, so against the worst odds, that even their destroyers stood in awe of them.

In 1949, the orchestra began disbanding. A number of the musicians planned to emigrate to Israel, my mother and her sister among them, possibly to reorganize the orchestra there. The sisters had already shipped their belongings ahead, including a piano. My father did not wish to go to Israel at this time, reluctant to enter another military environment. He had an aunt and uncle in Brooklyn, New York, who were sponsoring him there. He prevailed upon my mother to change her plans and come with him to New York. If they joined him, he promised to take care of both her and her sister. He left for America and, once he arrived, wrote her pleading letters. Meanwhile, my mother was traveling through Europe before returning to Germany. She loved my father, persuaded Henia, and they both joined him in New York, traveling on the U.S.S. General A. W. Greeley in late 1949-50.

During the ship's crossing, my aunt met her husband-to-be, Simon Gurko, and they married soon after their arrival. My father kept his word, and my parents' lives in America began.

Kultur-Amt bajm C. K. fun di Bafrajte Jdn in der U. S. Zone

dem   a zejger

In zal fun

**Reprezentanc
Orkester fun der
Szerit Haplejta**

Grojser Koncert

(In basztand fun 21 Perzon)

Dirigent:

E. BORSTEIN

Koncertmajster:

A. Stupel

Bajm Klavir:

Fanny Durmaszkin

Solisten:

Folkszingerin: Opernzingerin:

Henny Durmaszkin / Anny Stein

Tenor:

Georg Richter

In Program: Klasisze, idisze, hebreisze un geto muzik

Biletn cu bakumen in Kultur-Amt

Fania Durmashkin, my mother, and her sister, Henia,
performing with the Shearith Hapleitah Orchestra in 1949.

Fania and Max in Fürstenfeldbruck.

Chapter 6

Our Beginnings

This is my first memory. It was 1952, Brooklyn, New York. The pink crocheted blanket was tucked under my chin and the sky above was a brilliant blue painted with pure white, cottony clouds. The blanket was held in place by rounded silver cuffs on the carriage sides, like bracelets on a chain, engraved with my name. The view from overhead was cut off by the black cloth hood of the carriage. To the right, I could see the playground fence. I felt secure, curious, in wonder of life.

We lived on New Jersey Avenue in East New York, Brooklyn, where many Jewish Holocaust survivors had settled along with their hopes for a new life. Their first children were born in that neighborhood, as I was, in the Brooklyn Women's Hospital on Eastern Parkway.

My parents, my aunt, and I lived on the fourth floor in a three-room apartment in a small, turn-of-the-century building that was kept very clean. My paternal Aunt Lisa and Uncle Charles had lived there first, and moved to an apartment on the first floor so that my father, mother, and aunt could have their own place.

The rectangular, brick building had tiled floors, thickly painted walls and ceilings, and dimly lit hallways that reverberated with the sounds of tenants coming and going. Soon we were able to identify our neighbors by the pattern and texture of their steps. One of the first friends we made lived diagonally across the hall from us. Mrs. Weiss was a tiny elderly lady, slightly hunched over, with a cute little wrinkled face that reminded me of a walnut. I loved visiting her and looking at her old-fashioned keepsakes and photos of her children, which she loved to show off. She was from Eastern Europe, but I never learned her story. Whenever she baked apple pies, she would deliver one to our apartment, and soon became a surrogate grandmother right next door who treated me with kindness and love.

Our apartment had two bedrooms and an eat-in kitchen. The table sat next to a black upright piano. There was a four-legged white porcelain stove edged in black along the adjacent wall, and across from it was a deep porcelain double sink where my mother bathed me when I was tiny. Opposite the table there was a window overlooking treetops and tar roofs. The vista was diagonally slashed with gray clotheslines.

On some sunny days, my mother hung damp, freshly washed sheets out to dry on our clothesline–the pulley was right outside y parents' bedroom window. She opened the window wide, winter or summer, put the red flowered cloth bag of wooden clothes pins on the windowsill and hung the sheets, some white, some blue, pulling on the rope for more leverage as she went along, pegging the cloth expanses to the line every foot or so. The wind lifted and billowed them like sails that I imagined would navigate our family to different heavenly destinations. When they were dry, my mother gathered them in, reversing the process. She would call me over, scooping up an armful of the newly washed laundry, and let me watch as she put her face to the fabric, breathing in the scent of sunshine and air, inviting me to do the same. "See how fresh it smells," she said appreciatively. I, too, buried my face in the cloth, happy to share this moment with my mother.

But one day, the laundry ropes were empty. The sky was a leaden gray. My mother stood at her bedroom window looking out. Her back was to me. I called out to her. Once. Again. She didn't turn around. I realized then that she was in a place where I could not reach her, a profoundly private, compelling place from her past, and I discovered, at the age of three, that I was not always the center of her world.

The playground fence I had first seen from my carriage was on the corner of our block, right next door to the building. It contained swings, monkey bars, slides, and handball courts. I remember my mother taking me to the playground and slipping me into a small metal swing seat with a safety bar that slid into place in front of me. She would push the swing forward, and taught me to bend my little legs to gain momentum. I loved the feeling of flying as high as I could.

At that time, my mother had long, thick brown hair that she held back with a dark clip. Lipstick was the only makeup she ever wore. Her skin glowed, and her complexion was soft and fresh. When we went out to do errands or shop in the neighborhood, she greeted everyone and was greeted in turn by all our neighbors and local shopkeepers, who had great affection and respect for her. There was no elevator in the building, so she dragged her packages, regardless of their weight, up four steep flights of stairs. Eventually, she bought a shopping cart and walked backwards up the stairs, hauling her packages up to the apartment, one step at a time.

The dry cleaner had a shop next door to our building, and beside it was the classic corner candy store owned by Hy and Lily. It had red vinyl-covered stools that spun around in front of the long red soda fountain counter. Hy was king of his domain. Standing behind the counter as he shmoozed with his clients, he whipped up malteds and milk shakes, egg creams, ice cream sodas, and regular sodas from the colored syrups arrayed in square glass containers—orange, lime, lemon, pineapple, cherry, and cola—each with its own pump. Using a long, metal spoon he'd mix the ingredients with "2¢ plain" (seltzer from the tap) in tall Coca Cola glasses, with their trademarked curves. He would set the drinks in front of his customers as he chatted and checked on his two sons by looking out the window from the corner of his eye.

The jumbo jukebox, with its flashing lights and shiny chrome adornments, held a hundred 45 rpm records that were lifted onto the turntable by a robotic arm. It was filled with the musical hit parade of the '50s—Frank Sinatra, Dinah Shore, Tony Bennett, Rosemary Clooney, Perry Como, Buddy Holly, Elvis Presley, Connie Francis, and people we never heard from again—the stars we called the one-hit wonders. I loved chocolate malteds and pretzel sticks that were about a foot long, an inch thick, covered with rock salt and costing just two cents.

Across the street from the candy store was another classic: the grocery store owned by a Holocaust survivor. It was dark and musty, but carried all the basic products you could possibly need except for fresh baked goods: Pechter's cellophane wrapped pumpernickel, butter, eggs, cream cheese, sardines, lox, herring, and other goodies. You were greeted by the garlicky, briny smell from the huge pickle barrel outside the door. Often, the owner would hand me a sour or half-sour pickle if I came in with my mom. We knew his days were numbered after the A&P supermarket opened a block away under the Pitkin Avenue El (the Els are the elevated subway tracks that still run through various parts of New York City).

The kosher butcher was on the next block. Having a butcher nearby meant you were truly living in a Jewish community. He had crates of live chickens delivered to his store, where he'd ritually slaughter them himself—and he was carefully trained and trusted to do this work correctly, or people who kept kosher would not eat the meat.

My mother would buy chicken, lamb chops, chopped meat, steaks, and roasts, all freshly cut or ground to order. The shop's wooden floor was covered with sawdust, and the butcher's once-white apron was always smeared with blood, as was his solid, heavy wood chopping block. After bringing the meat home, my mother would put it in the sink in large pots full of water, cover the meat with salt, and then soak it for several hours so that no blood remained. Everything was always bought fresh because our freezers were tiny and could hold very little.

Today, when we want to repair worn out shoes, we have a tough time finding a shoemaker, but when I was growing up, shoes were expensive, and there were shoe repair shops in every neighborhood. The place we frequented was an old shop on Sutter Avenue owned by an elderly, Jewish immigrant with a raspy voice who wore his wire-rimmed glasses way down on his nose. We called him *Der Schuster* (The Shoemaker). He was a heavy smoker and his head was always wreathed in a tobacco fog whose scent was mixed with the pungent smell of freshly tanned leather, glue, and shoe polish. His counter was always piled high with worn shoes–from fancy dress slippers to the humblest down-at-the-heels work shoes.

He loved our company, and enjoyed speaking Yiddish with my mother while we waited for him to repair our shoes. Along the wall opposite the work counter, the Schuster had installed a row of waist-high wooden booths with swinging doors where customers sat and shmoozed with him while they too waited for their shoes. These were three connected "boxes," each about four-foot square with a wooden seat facing him. The seats' armrests contained small, metal ashtrays and I loved opening the squeaky wooden doors and sitting in the cozy cubbyhole while my shoes were being fixed.

I started kindergarten when I was five years old. My parents specifically wanted me to attend the local public school. "She's an American," said my Papa, because public school represented multi-faceted American society. A few years later, I was sent to Talmud Torah (afternoon Hebrew school), when my public school day ended. It was located in an old synagogue, and at 3:30 p.m., four days a week, our dingy classroom filled up with reluctant kids whose parents wanted them to study Judaism and Hebrew.

I don't remember if I was reluctant. I do remember a Mrs. Tova who tried to teach us basic reading and writing. She wore dark, modest dresses and was always cheerful. I loved the small notebooks with blue-lined pages configured to accommodate Hebrew letters–one thin space for the letters with a wider space underneath for the vowels. Eventually, I finished the course, and what I learned there has remained with me. I read Hebrew more quickly today than I did then, and I attribute my important introduction to the small, bare classroom and Mrs. Tova's cheerful lessons. When I was a little older, my parents hired a religious high school girl, Batya, as a private Hebrew tutor for me. She became my role model because she was bright, patient, funny, and always offered me the mint gum she favored and constantly chewed.

My education was not confined solely to the classroom. As culture buffs familiar with cosmopolitan life in Europe before the war, my parents knew how to take full advantage of New York City's museums, theaters, and concert halls, especially on weekends—and they often brought me along. Radio City Music Hall was a regular treat around holiday time. We also visited the Metropolitan Museum of Art and the Museum of Natural History with its dinosaurs and prehistoric dioramas of the Cro-Magnon era. We went to the Philharmonic, and I especially loved the ballet. We enjoyed the Bolshoi and Moiseyev Ballet companies from Russia and the New York City Ballet. By the time I was a teenager, I had seen *Swan Lake, Sleeping Beauty*, and *The Nutcracker Suite* several times.

My father, an accomplished violinist, adored Tchaikovsky and had performed his concertos in Europe. When he brought me to Manhattan, he made me feel like a princess, especially when we watched the ballerinas in Swan Lake. I believe that this early exposure to the arts—and learning how to play a musical instrument at a young age—deeply influenced the way I look at life. As a child, I felt that I was privileged to belong to a rarefied world linked to my parents' historic past and heritage, a family tradition that pre-dated the war.

In America, that talent played itself out in my great-aunt's family. My mother's aunt was Tillie Grace Durmashkin, who married my mother's paternal uncle, Mordechai. One day, as the story was told, he up and deserted the family, and moved to Brighton Beach, Brooklyn, where he lived alone. He was *persona non grata* for that and also because in 1939 he turned down a request from the famous cantor, Moshe Koussevitsky, to assist my mother's brother, Wolf

Durmashkin, a brilliant musician from Vilna, by sponsoring his immigration to the U.S.

Tante (Aunt) Grace raised her three daughters on her own. One of them, Henny Damur, became a Broadway and Hollywood actress in the 1930s. Another, Hannah, married a lovely gentleman, Bill, who worked for the U.S. State Department. They traveled a great deal. The third daughter, Sarah, was a pianist.

Tante Grace and Sarah were quite close to my parents, and Sarah visited from time to time. During her visits she liked to see how I was progressing musically. One day, to test my sense of pitch, she put a white cloth over the piano keyboard and randomly played notes one at a time. I identified the notes correctly because I could see the outlines of the keys against the cloth. I never let on, because I was embarrassed, so both she and my mother thought I had perfect pitch!

At about the time I started kindergarten, my parents began spending summers in a Rockaway Beach boarding house one block from the Atlantic Ocean. We rented one bedroom and shared a kitchen with other families who were there for the summer. The kitchen held six old-fashioned, four-legged porcelain stoves like the one in our apartment on New Jersey Avenue. We brought some pots and pans with us, and Mom would use one of the stoves to cook our meals. During the day I spent hours on the beach with other children, swimming and body-surfing in the salty, blue-gray Atlantic, burrowing tunnels, building sand castles, and digging for small gray sand crabs to play with.

Like all the other fathers, during the week my father stayed in the hot, humid city—there was little air-conditioning in those days. He went to work on crowded, steamy subways and when he finally got home after spending the day on the hot cutting-room floor, sweating on the samples and piece goods, he would cool off at home by sitting down in front of a free-standing, rotating fan. Friday afternoons were fraught with anticipation as I happily awaited his arrival, peering down the block from my post at the outside gate.

Tillie Grace Durmashkin.

Henny Damur.

Sarah Durmashkin.

Hannah Durmashkin.

When I'd spot him, I would run to him for the biggest hug he could give me, and to receive the small gift he usually brought. We spent the weekends together as a family, going to the beach, relaxing in lounge chairs or porch rocking chairs on the large veranda, and going for strolls on the boardwalk. Those were happy, carefree times for us.

When I was six, my mother began to teach me how to play the piano on the old black upright we had in the kitchen. It had a narrow mirror across the top that reflected the light from the kitchen window.

I had a daily schedule: I'd come home from school, go out and play with my friends for an hour, come home and practice piano for an hour, then do my homework. Although I would have liked to stay out longer with my friends, I felt the importance of the musical connection. It was part of my family history, a key to deeper life awareness, to tragic loss in my family's background, and to its essence and identity. I knew I played a role in all that, but I was still way too young to understand or identify it. I felt apart from other children my age. I couldn't go outside for unlimited play and was subject to an imposed discipline that I didn't necessarily welcome. Nonetheless, I was aware that music connected me to a larger world beyond the alleyways, hopscotch grids, and backyards of our Brooklyn neighborhood. I yearned to be fully part of that world one day.

Mom was the person who brought me to the library for the very first time. I must have been seven years old, and I was hooked from then on. Books opened new worlds and introduced me to fascinating people. They became friends and family members. I discovered nuances of emotion, and developed levels of sensitivity towards people that I might otherwise have missed. Novels and biographies were my favorites, and I began to write poetry. It seemed an appropriate avocation, since our home life was steeped in music and words, poetry, and classic literature.

I remember one poignant, sweet moment, when I was in the third grade and came home for lunch one day. I found my mother dressed in a straight, light-blue skirt and short-sleeved white blouse. By then her hair was short, already gray and pinned back from her face. The front fell forward a bit in a flattering curve on her forehead. Her eyes were blue-gray and she was wearing dark pink lipstick. She smelled fresh, clean, and fragrant, like a meadow of flowers. I'd just learned about Abraham Lincoln, and was chattering to her about his life as she put some boxes away in a closet. She was half-listening. Finally, I reached the point of Lincoln's assassination and exclaimed dramatically, "And, as he sat in the theater with his wife, he was shot in the head!" My mother turned to me with a stricken look on her face, and said in Yiddish, "Oh, no! The poor little bird."

On holidays like Passover and on weekends, we often visited my Aunt Henia, Uncle Simon, and my cousins, Vivian, Rita, and Abe, in their large old house in Weehawken, New Jersey. I loved spending time with the kids, especially because I was an only child. We played games and created pretend worlds and scenarios endlessly. Our parents enjoyed these visits, too. They sat at the large dining room table, peeling and eating fruit, sipping tea, nibbling on sponge cake and cracked nuts, laughing at stories we kids didn't pay attention to. We took it for granted that we were all the family that remained from whatever had been before. None of us questioned the absence of grandparents, other uncles, aunts, and cousins.

When it was time to go home, leaving my cousins seemed unthinkable to me. But, before it got too dark, my mom and I would climb into my dad's 1957 Plymouth Belvedere–coral and cream-colored–and we would drive back to Brooklyn. I couldn't wait for our next visit.

Also in my sixth year, I was looking through my parents' chest of drawers one day, curiously examining my mother's jewelry, my father's cuff links, and some sparkling, jeweled buttons. Then, I found them. Packs of photos printed on ordinary paper, now brown with time, captioned in German. The images confirmed my parents' stories. There were mountains of corpses with their mouths open; bodies laid out after an execution. An elderly Jewish man stands with glazed eyes looking at the camera. On his left is a German soldier cutting the old man's beard with a scissor. On his right is another German soldier with the barrel of a pistol held to the elderly man's head. Both soldiers are laughing uproariously. There are photos of children shot en masse, their faces so clear and beautiful, reflecting their last thoughts of parents, toys, and friends. They seem almost alive in gentle sleep.

What do these photos say to me? They tell me that the world is not a safe, secure cocoon. Where did they come from? I imagine one of my parents got them after the war, perhaps during their DP years, when the shocking contents of the Nazis' own archives began surfacing publicly. These photos are the visual evidence of my parents' memories, of events from their teenage and young adult lives. I am so wracked with horror and pity I push the reality off and put the photos away. But the disturbing images continued to haunt me.

When I was about nine years old, we discovered the Catskill Mountains and went to a bungalow colony where other Holocaust survivors were renting bungalows, too, and that included my aunt and uncle and their kids. Each family had its own bungalow, which consisted of an eat-in kitchen, one or two bedrooms, a bathroom, and usually, a small, screened porch.

Every family there had kids, most of them my age, and we spent the day inventing games and waiting with excitement for the peddlers who would arrive with their carloads of merchandise. The fruit man would drive up in an open truck laden with fresh produce, and there was one fellow who sold nothing but women's blouses out of his car. We kids were so busy with ourselves, our mothers only saw us during mealtimes. The best times were the trips into Monticello, the closest town, with its wide Main Street that began at the firehouse. I loved going in with my mom, who would take me to the kosher butcher and then treat me to a hand-dipped ice cream cone at the candy store.

Fathers came up on weekends. We called them the working warriors, and they would carpool from Brooklyn to Monticello via the old Route 17, a ride that in those days could take four long hours.

They looked forward to Saturday night, the night out for the parents. Dotted through the mountains were the hotels that bred the funniest stand-up comics in America. The best hotels had elaborate nightclubs, and our parents would doll themselves up in their finest clothes to go "clubbing" in the old-fashioned sense. They would catch the shows at the Concord, Brown's, the Stevensville, Kutsher's, and the Nevele. Jerry Lewis, Buddy Hackett, Jan Peerce, Jan Murray, Jack Benny, Phil Silvers, Johnny Carson, Jackie Mason—it was amazing who was there!

The teenagers in each bungalow colony got together, found a ride, and would head to the best show for the night, to see if they could get in to meet members of the opposite sex. Many future doctors were waiting tables and cleaning swimming pools for the tips to pay their way through medical school. Those were sweet and nostalgic times, but I must admit that my favorite moments were spent with my nose buried in books as well as living out fantasy worlds in the woods with my friends. As much as I adored the companionship of our playgroup, I just loved to read, and in the cultural climate of our home, it was as natural as music.

Chapter 7
The Sound of Music

Music permeated our home. I remember evenings when friends gathered at our home and my parents played tangos and popular melodies from their youth. They also performed at gatherings of the society from their native city, Nusach Vilne. In 1962, my mother and aunt Henia made a record of ghetto songs, *Songs to Remember,* which is still available on CD.

My mother loved to play the piano, and my father often accompanied her on his violin. When she played solo, her favorite pieces were Chopin's etudes and waltzes. I watched her fingers fly across the keyboard as she sat and swayed with emotion. When my parents weren't playing, there was still music in the air, since the old radio was always tuned to WQXR, the *New York Times'* classical music station. My parents would listen with rapt attention to broadcasts of symphonies and concertos.

What a treat it was whenever my father took his violin case out of the closet in the bedroom, put it on the bed, and opened it! The case was lined in rich, purple velvet. My father would pull back the purple velvet covering, and there it was! The shiny mahogany-colored violin lay there like a valuable jewel, a pampered baby in its regal carriage! Inside were more treasures. The case had small compartments that pulled open to reveal violin strings rolled in flat crackling envelopes marked with German writing; a worn chin cushion; extra string-tightening pegs, and a hard block of resin for rubbing against the bowstrings, which had their own fitted sections in the case's cover.

Then came the moments I loved best of all. My father would tuck the little cushion under his chin, slightly incline it to the right, delicately lift the violin out of its velvet bed and place it against the cushion and his chin, then begin plucking the strings to hear if they were in tune. He'd choose a bow and would ceremoniously begin the tuning ritual, listening intently for the correct pitch. When all the adjustments were made, he would pause and then begin to play. Beethoven. Tchaikovsky. A tango. A Gypsy melody. He played it all with delicacy, concentration, and dexterity. He would transport me to realms of beauty where he was totally at one with himself, beyond the boundaries of our three-room apartment and the limits of time.

When my father arrived in the U.S. in 1949, he tried to pursue his career as a violinist, but had to shift gears professionally in anticipation of the arrival of my mother and her sister, both of whom he planned to support. He eventually became a cutter and grader of ladies' coats and suits in Manhattan's garment district. He was much sought after because of his skills, his pleasant, respectful manner, and his industriousness. He worked hard and took advantage of long hours of overtime. As a child, I rarely saw him, except on Saturday nights and Sundays. He'd normally come home long after my bedtime. On an occasional late night, I'd wake up and hear my mother open and close the front door. They would whisper as my Papa came in and I'd fall back asleep, feeling comforted and secure, knowing he was home.

My father once told me a story about his first job in the U.S. in 1950. He was told if he wanted to be a violinist, he'd have to join the musicians' union, so one morning he took the subway to the union hall. The lines of out-of-work musicians stretched around the block and he realized immediately that finding a viable musician's post would be a remote possibility, perhaps one not worth pursuing, since he had to support a new wife, a baby on its way, and his sister-in-law as well. He needed a job with a regular salary. So, he followed in the footsteps of my great-Uncle Charles, who was in the garment industry.

Initially, Papa got a job sewing shoes together. With no training whatsoever, he was asked to operate a sewing machine and was given shoe parts to assemble. A kindly, Italian-American working next to him watched for a while as my father, soaked in sweat from the effort, tried and tried to operate the machine. Finally, the gentleman came over to help him. "America, I Love You," the man sang ironically as he gave my father some helpful tips.

Once, when I'd bought a new jacket, my father asked to look at it. Because he worked for high-end manufacturers, he was proud of his reputation and was the family expert on judging a good garment. First, he fingered the wool cloth. "Not bad," he murmured, which meant it was good. Then, he opened the jacket and examined the lining. "This material is not so great," he commented. Then he looked carefully at the buttonholes. "Not hand sewn like buttonholes used to be, but strong enough."

I always regarded my father as a true judge of quality. This came through in his music and in his work. Like my mother, who was meticulous in every task—housework, cooking, playing the piano— my father was also thorough and paid great attention to detail. In their bedroom closet, their clothes were hung perfectly, covered by plastic bags from the dry cleaners. Other clothing was beautifully folded in their dresser drawers. They were quite stylish and tasteful in their apparel choices. I loved to watch them take out their fancy clothes as they prepared for a gala evening. The air was filled with my mother's perfume—Chanel Number 5 or Nina Ricci—and my Papa's aftershave. He would help her zip up the back of her dress and click closed the clasp of her gold charm bracelet. My mother's hats, gloves, and purses were color-coordinated, and she looked so elegant! My father looked dapper in his charcoal-gray suits and hats. Later on, when he was more established in the garment district, he brought home marvelous coats and suits for my mother and me. The fabrics and colors were excellent, and the styles were couture level.

That is how I learned early on about the meaning of quality. Good quality is not only about what is pleasing on the surface. As a young child, when I listened to my parents' music, I experienced the transcendent world they created for themselves and their listeners, an expansive and wonderful world that touched everyone who heard them.

Awareness of quality is a double-edged sword. As an only child, I was, perhaps, more lonely, but also somewhat more adult. I had only a few friends, but very close ones. I learned that true connection is precious and rare. But the process of obtaining it also enhances its value. This holds true whether you're looking for a friend, a new jacket, or an intimate relationship. This lesson I learned from my parents has stayed with me my whole life.

We moved from East New York to Sheepshead Bay, Brooklyn, when I was eleven. It was a milestone for my parents– they'd purchased their first house. It was a modest home, an attached brick, two-family house identical to every house on the block…but it was my mother's palace. There was a washer and dryer in the basement. There was a backyard and a garage. All the furniture and appliances were bought new. There was a porch where my parents would sit on warm spring evenings. And that was pretty much how the house remained for the next 45 years. My parents took immaculate care of their possessions. My mother cleaned and polished until all the surfaces shone. When my father bought a new champagne-colored 1967 Pontiac Tempest, he cared for it as if it were alive. It lasted for twenty-five years. Drivers on the road used to stop and gawk, asking how much my Papa wanted for it. But he'd never sell it.

I was an English major and loved literature. When I was in college I was offered an opportunity to spend my junior year at a British university and I jumped at the chance. I discussed the idea with my parents and, although they agreed, I could sense they were not enthusiastic. After all, I was their only child, and we'd never been separated to this extent before.

Because of my family's Holocaust legacy and musical background, I'd always felt different from my classmates and more sheltered than they were. My parents' life view, although optimistic, had been tainted with sadness and mistrust from their tragic past. Now, as a young adult, I finally had the opportunity to explore the world. I also had an unconscious mission –*tikkun olam*, to repair that world and experience joy beyond my Brooklyn boundaries.

Before I left for England, I sat down with my mom one afternoon. Her gentle, almost child-like, blue-gray eyes studied me for a few moments. "The world is really a beautiful place, full of wonders," she said. "And as much as people can make the world wonderful, some of them can also ruin it for everyone."

I stayed at the university in England for two years. During the second year, I continued my studies and became the au pair for the vice chancellor's little boy. The family was gracious, and I was able to transfer a certain number of credits to my college at home. I graduated in January.

Back in New York, I took a job in book publishing for about a year, and then decided to get my master's degree in English and American literature at another university in England. During that year, I lived in an 18th-century cottage in the countryside with other students. I traveled, studied, and was introduced to the profession of teaching English to non-English speakers. I completed my year, and then returned to New York, where I applied for another master's degree in teaching English as a Second Language. I was accepted at a marvelous school in Vermont that specialized in promoting cross-cultural communication. The students were from all over the world, and the atmosphere was exactly what I was looking for. During our three months of student teaching practice, I lived and worked in Mexico, spending time in Veracruz and Atlixco, while living with local families. Armed with my new credentials, I taught briefly in Boston, then applied for jobs in Japan. I landed an opportunity in Osaka. After about nine months there, I changed jobs and moved to Tokyo. And that's where I remained for the next four years.

My time overseas was full of adventure, and I made several visits home. Much to their credit, my parents accepted my absence graciously, although I know it pained them. Ultimately, they were quite proud of me, even though they really wanted me to just settle down, get married to a successful Jewish man, and have a family. I pay tribute to their love and honor for me, which touched and protected me no matter where I was in the world...and still does.

By now I was settled in my New York life, but all was not well. By degrees, my mother began exhibiting erratic, aggressive behavior. We took her to doctors for testing, and our fears were confirmed: She had Alzheimer's disease. She stayed at home with my father as long as possible.

In 1993, my father and I were supposed to take her for a more definitive test. He was always meticulously early for appointments, but that day he didn't show up. I raced to their home, and found my mother extremely confused, asking over and over again where my father was. A policeman had been to the house and left an accident report. When I called the precinct, I was told my father was in the hospital after he'd lost consciousness at the wheel of his car and driven into a school bus. I was on the verge of hysterics, but channeled my energy into action. I took my mother and we went to the hospital to find him. He was awake, but had to have bypass surgery because clogged arteries had caused him to black out. Once the surgery was performed, he came home to recuperate, necessitating the hiring of a professional caretaker.

This created great conflict for my mother, father, and Lucy, the nurse. My mother's aggressive behavior was directed at Lucy and sometimes at me. We consulted with medical professionals and social workers. With a great deal of pain and weeping, my father and I decided that we would place my mother in a home that specialized in caring for people in her condition. It was an act of spiritual and physical amputation and we never stopped mourning our decision, though we deemed it necessary for all of us.

The day she left our home, I had to call an ambulance to bring her to a hospital on Staten Island for initial testing. I told her I was going for a ride with her. She accepted my explanation and went quietly. I left my father in tears and took her downstairs. She turned for a last look at the house, as if she knew. It took all my strength not to break down. I was betraying her! How could I be responsible for taking her away from her home?

When we finally arrived at the hospital, the staff kindly and competently took over, and soon I had to leave. As they took her to another room, she looked at me over her shoulder, her face wistful, like a baffled child. It was deep winter and the streets were dark and icy. I walked towards the ferry, sobbing out loud, my heart broken. When I called the next morning to ask after her, I was told she'd played the piano in the recreation room and that she'd also spent hours sitting in a chair in front of the elevators, waiting. When I told my father, he and I both began to cry.

He said, "It's like the story she told about her family's cat that stayed outside the door waiting for them to return after the Nazis took them. She stayed like that, waiting for them, until the day she died." It was unbearable. Mom was in the hospital for a couple of days. I went to see her, and then accompanied her to the nursing home. She never came home again.

My mother died in 1998 after a lengthy struggle with Alzheimer's and the physical deterioration that accompanies it, as did her sister in 2002. The disease was cruel, but the shock of losing Mama reverberated with us for years and is something you never get over.

She was in the nursing home for four and a half years. My father visited her daily. He'd spend the entire day sitting at her side until she was put to bed at night. In the third year of her illness, as she grew more childlike and remote, she suddenly refused to eat. The doctors said she'd have to get a feeding tube.

My father was beside himself and refused to allow it. He sat for hours, cajoling her to eat. He brought her favorite fruits, cut them into small pieces and held them to her mouth with a spoon, whispering sweet endearments in Yiddish, as if he were feeding a small bird.

Finally, after days of patiently holding spoons of food to her mouth, she ate some of the fruit! The doctors were amazed at his persistence and her response. How could they know about the exquisite, caring heart that resided in my small, Jewish father? How could they know that his love for us was boundless, and that, in this love, he was also caring for his murdered parents and six beloved sisters and brothers? How could they know how he gave us all of himself, but suffered daily for the lost ones? How could they ever know?

Several years passed. My father grew more elderly and frail, but maintained himself immaculately and opted to remain in his home, although we discussed other options from time to time. He was alert, though sometimes a bit forgetful. Nevertheless, he maintained a lively interest in people, his surroundings and a keen sense of humor. He would ask me if I needed money. Reaching into his pocket for his wallet, my 5'3" father would ask me, "Sonia, are you short?"

"Well, Dad, you know I'm a little short, but how about you?" I'd laugh.

"If I had a million dollars, I'd still be short," he quipped with that mischievous smile that always lit up his face.

Then he told me a story about one of his excursions to Brighton Beach to view the neighborhood and to look for bargains. As he stood there waiting on the subway platform wearing his signature Kangol cap, a tall, young policeman standing next to him suddenly began sneezing violently and just couldn't stop. My father looked up at him calmly and asked, "Whatsa' matter? Shoes too tight?"

The policeman burst into laughter and stopped sneezing. They both enjoyed the joke.

Then, one day, on his way to mail me a letter, he fell and hit his head on the sidewalk. From then on, he was in and out of hospitals and nursing homes.

In early spring 2005, the view from the window of his bedroom showed a tree beginning to sprout pink buds. My father had been in this nursing home bed for six months now. Blue tracheostomy tubes were connected to his throat from a hissing oxygen tank. When I came into the room, he sensed it immediately. "Daddy!" I called out. "Mameleh," his lips formed the endearment. He could not speak. He could not eat, and had a feeding tube in his stomach. He lifted his skinny arms and I ran to embrace him. He was so thin in my arms! I loved to feel his warm cheek against mine. We gazed at each other with unrestrained love, and showered each other with kisses. Although my heart and mind screamed with desperation for his healing, I knew how tenuous his hold on life really was.

"Please, please, Papa, don't give up."

"I'm trying, *Mameleh*, I'm trying," he mouthed. In those moments, my father and I lived in an eternal dimension. There, blessed by God, I felt love without end in the warmth of my father's hazel eyes. I was privileged to share those moments with him. They were and are a treasure beyond price.

Soon my father was strong enough to use a speaking tube, a small, round device that fit over the plastic hole in his throat and enabled him to talk. It was a joy to hear his voice again and speak with him about how he felt, what was happening in the world, the weather, jokes, anything at all. One morning, a nurse entered the room, and he gave her a cheery compliment, "You look very nice today!"

"Why, thank you, Max!" she replied. "Why is it that you're never grumpy or bad-tempered like so many other people here? You just never complain!"

"My dear," he said, lifting his finger for emphasis, "I was a human being when I was a young man, and I'm a human being now that I'm old."

One afternoon, as I sat beside him, he looked over at me and asked, "Where's Mommy?" meaning, my mother. "When is she coming? And where are my sisters, Rochele and Perele, and the other children? Are they still in school?"

My heart was pierced with unspeakable pain. I assured him that my mother would be there soon, and that the children were just fine. I held his hand and turned my head towards the window so he could not see my bitter tears.

Chapter 8
The Empty Home

The key clicked the lock open easily, but the door resisted. I pushed hard, and it gave way as if to say, "Opening this isn't difficult. You just have to know how." The odor of the house embraced me with the lingering scents of my adolescence– my dad's woodsy aftershave, my mom's fresh-flower cologne, the residual smell of the immaculate 1967 Pontiac Tempest in the orderly garage. It was a house that had been cleaned and sparkled by my mother's loving hand for almost 45 years.

All the furniture was gone now, and my footsteps echoed in the rooms. Memories suffused the air. I remembered my mother at the Baldwin baby grand piano, my papa with his violin, playing a tango for their friends from Europe, enjoying the songs of their distant young days. Mom would sometimes ask me to play a Chopin nocturne or a Mozart sonata for their guests, and I would fight my performance nervousness to oblige her.

In the now empty kitchen, the air carried the hints of aromas from holiday meals of soft brisket, hearty potato kugel, moist chicken, and celestial chicken soup–delicious results of my mother's labors of love. I watched the dust motes waltz through the sunlight that poured in through the dinette window. Could these dancing particles have absorbed some of my family's essence through their constant presence and reprocessing for 45 years? I caught a few on my open palm and rubbed them against my cheek. Perhaps my father's last solitary years were absorbed into these molecules, and I wanted to hold him against my face again. I began to cry, and each tear was like a word on a page, like a snapshot of the living past, recalling a story that needs to be told.

The horrors of the past cannot be made less horrible, but they can be shared. They can touch our hearts and teach us about dignity, respect, tolerance and the endurance of the human spirit. My father, Max Beker, was a human being par excellence, a gentleman of the old school, a man of honor and pride, a loving family man. At the age of 88, his soul left us and finally joined my mother, his parents, sisters and brothers, and they are together at last.

Epilogue

When I arrived there in May 2006, Vilna was just edging into the lushness of spring. Everywhere, the city was full of the sweet scent of purple, blossoming lilac trees. The population was well-dressed, courteous, and pleasant. Couples and families strolled slowly through the quaint streets, enjoying small restaurants and cafés. Students rushed past the entrance to the university, which has stood there for hundreds of years. The renaissance of this medieval city is partially due to the student population. Certain streets contain small art galleries and art supply shops run by students. A number of the bars and internet cafés are frequented by students as well. Student graffiti also appears on newly-painted walls, much of it in English: "Your life will be happy and peaceful, only for 99.99%" and "The important thing is to express yourself."

The house where the Beker family lived—and from where they were torn and herded to Ponary to be shot—is on such a street. Paupio is under gentrification and is two blocks from the peaceful, picturesque Vilaika River. The street goes downhill and ends in a small copse of trees. When I was there for the first time with my excellent guide, Regina, I asked her, "Do you think my father knew this part of the street?" "Oh, yes, I'm sure," she answered. "He knew it, and it knew him."

It was not a prosperous area when my father and his family lived there. I walked in from the street, under the arch, over the damp cobblestones leading to my paternal ancestral home. I admired the small flower garden in the courtyard center, and gazed at the apartment door. I imagined my family's voices and thoughts. I let them know how much I loved my father, their son, and brother, and what a truly wonderful man he turned out to be. Then I was choked by tears and grief.

In another part of town, my mother's house, on Mindaugines St. (formerly Shevchenko), is an odd, free-standing, two-story structure set back on an angle from the street, occupying a wide grassy space. It is dilapidated, but must have once been elegant, judging from the decorative tracery along the side of the building. Regina, fearless guide and Jewish genealogist, knocked on the door of Apartment 5, where my maternal ancestors, the Durmashkins once lived. I felt my stomach lurch as we entered a blackened, shared kitchen area, then walked further to a room occupied by an elderly couple.

Bright with daylight that was streaming in through two tall windows, on one wall is a small metal door in a tiled, enclosed chimney. I imagined that this must have been one of the piano rooms where my mother and her brother would practice, and where my grandmother burned coal or wood in the stove during the bitter cold winters. In the back of the house is a garden, and I caught my breath as I remembered my mother's story of how her brother, fearing that the Nazis would snatch him from the house, suggested leaving a rope hanging from the third story window so he could quickly lower himself into the garden and run away through the side street. I saw it in front of my eyes, their tender hopes and dreams, their struggles and longing to stay alive and together—hopes so cruelly dashed.

One rainy afternoon, my talented friend, Marija Krupoves, a popular folk singer when she isn't a professor at Vilnius University's Yiddish Institute in the Department of Stateless Cultures, gave a concert at Vilnius's Franciscan Church. A small, rapt audience contained a group of Marija's Franciscan monk friends. Accompanied by a violin and bass fiddle, she stood on a small stage under an enormous gold cross elevated above her head.

As her repertoire is international, she suddenly segued into the tender Yiddish song, "Ich Hob Dir Tzu Fiel Lieb," then into a lively Sephardi rendition of "Tzur Mishelo," ending with the Ladino "Avraham Avinu." By this time, the audience was clapping its hands and stomping its feet, the monks most enthusiastically of all.

Vilnius was redolent with paradoxes like this. At a birthday celebration for Dovid Katz, Vilnius University's Yiddish Institute scholar and professor, I was approached by a young woman who, in halting English, requested if she could interview me for the local Jewish TV show, Menorah. When I asked why, she told me that it was because I was Wolf Durmashkin's niece. I was abashed and said, "I'm so far from my uncle's greatness. Why me?" But the remnant of the survivors seemed so thrilled and happy that a Durmashkin family member had emerged from the Churban (destruction), that my visit was an appropriate occasion for all of us just to celebrate being together.

The first steps toward the establishment of a new Jewish community in Lithuania were taken in 1989 by the founding of the Association of the Culture of Lithuanian Jews. As of November 1991, it became the new Jewish Community of the Jews in Lithuania. The community is governed by the Community's Council, which is elected by the Conference along with the chairperson of the Community.

The Jewish population of Lithuania is estimated at some 5,000 (6,000 in 1997), most of them living in Vilnius.

"The Community...gives special attention to maintaining Jewish national identity, restoring religious life and the Jewish cultural heritage. It organizes meetings, lectures and exhibitions dedicated to an array of subjects including Israel and the Jewish holidays. Remembering Holocaust victims remains a top priority: there are over 200 places of mass extermination on the Lithuanian territory that need to be cared for."[53]

The Durmashkin home in present-day Vilnius.

The Beker home in present-day Vilnius.

The Jewish Gaon State Museum, founded in 1989, also has a permanent exhibition on the Holocaust and among various temporary exhibitions, "The Jews of Lithuania in the Fight against Nazism" opened in 2000, marking the fifty-fifth anniversary of the victory against the Nazis. Also, a list of the Vilna ghetto prisoners was published in a new book."[54] The Museum is also working on a large catalog that will feature the two hundred and eighty Vilna ghetto posters located in the City Archive, and a compendium identifying and discussing all the individuals featured in those posters.

The Community oversees cultural institutions, children's and youth clubs, and a senior center. It also publishes a four-language periodical. There is a Jewish school in Vilnius–the Shalom Aleichem State School–that has about 200 students. The Chabad community in Vilnius runs a private religious school. There is also a welfare program that supports pensioners in need and other impoverished people. This program is supported by Jewish organizations like the American Joint Distribution Committee and private contributions.

On another day, Stefan, my Vilna guide par excellence, hired a car to take us to Ponary. It was a visit I dreaded, but one which I had to make. As we drove out of the city, Stefan told me that just beyond the road were the railway tracks where thousands of hapless Vilna Jews from Lukiszki Prison were loaded onto freight cars and told by the Nazis they were going to be reunited with their families or taken to work. The train stopped at Ponary, and suddenly everyone knew it was the last stop. Pandemonium would break out, screaming people attempted to escape, ripping up the boxcars to get out. But their efforts came to nothing. Thousands of other Jews were forced to walk along the train tracks to Ponary, five miles from Vilna. They were executed there and buried in the seven pits left by the Russians.

Stefan told me that towards the end of the war, when the Nazis knew they were losing, they selected seventy Jews from a work camp outside the city, brought them to Ponary, put chains on their ankles and ordered them to dig up the bodies, burn them, pulverize the bones and then scatter the ashes. These people were housed in one of the pits that was lined with concrete. Often, they would find their dead family members and friends in the pits they were cleaning out. This gruesome work went on for three months. During this time, these seventy unfortunates carefully dug a small escape tunnel through one side of the pit, using spoons or other small metal implements they found in the clothes of the bodies. When they finally got through one night, they found they were very close to some Nazi guards. The group decided to run for it anyway. Eleven survived and found their way to the partisans.

Today, Ponary is peaceful and verdant, full of towering trees and soft, fertile earth. On the trip I took to research this book, I stood by one of the pits saying Kaddish and weeping. Stefan, my Lithuanian guide, stood behind me, waiting respectfully. When I was finished, he came over and handed me a small, delicate white flower with green leaves on its stem. "This is a flower from a strawberry plant. Very soon, this whole area will be covered with strawberries." He looked at me quietly and I looked back at him. We both understood what that flower meant, that it had grown and nourished itself from the blood-drenched soil. I took the flower carefully. Later, I pressed it into a book. Now, it is beautifully framed, hanging on my wall, and possibly contains thousands of Vilna's Jewish souls.[56]

The next day, Stefan and I strolled down fashionable Didzioji Street and made a left on Rudninku. We walked down this walled block and Stefan stopped in front of a large archway leading to a cobbled courtyard. Inside was a stone stairway that led to a set of ornate wooden doors. "This was the headquarters of the *Jüdenrat*," he said quietly. Before the war, the building had been a Yiddish gymnasium (high school) and is now a state-run architectural design and renovation center. A small plaque near the top of the arch designates its former purpose.

Throughout the Old Town of Vilnius, there are tastefully placed, gray stone plaques that label the places of the lost Jews—the ghetto gates, the location of the FPO uprising, the Great Synagogue, the Vilna Gaon's home, YIVO headquarters, the site of the former old

One of the many plaques throughout Vilna
commemorating its Jewish heritage. Both Akiva and Wolf
Durmashkin taught music at this school, now the site of the
Vilna Gaon Jewish State Museum.

cemetery, 1487–1950, destroyed by the Soviets to build a sports facility, the Strashun Library, the ghetto theater–all are in Yiddish and Lithuanian, sometimes in English. The placement of these monuments resulted from collaborative efforts between Vilnius's small, loyal, and tireless Jewish community and Jewish groups abroad. They appropriately mark buildings and commemorate events exactly where they occurred, and most are above eye level. The plaques in the Old Town blend into the stone buildings they adorn, and are easy to miss. Seemingly, they are a comment from the local population who tolerate and mildly encourage the recognition of the vibrant and vocal Jews who once lived in Vilna–but don't wish the memory to be too intrusive.

On Glazer Gass (Glass Street) some buildings retain a few hand-lettered signs in Yiddish that mark where there were stores that touted their wares from the pre-war period, and these are retouched when needed. Passing a quaint building, I saw underneath the sign, in a dark doorway, a local teenage couple clutch each other in passionate embrace. On Strashun, on the broken exposed wall of a second-story building a few feet down from the house where my mother and her family lived in the ghetto, is a frantically-carved Star of David. As I walked down Strashun with Regina, she showed me an old photo of the street we were on, and an elderly woman passing by muttered something to her. "What did she say?" I asked. "Oh, she just said, 'Jews, Jews', but she was being friendly." On the wall of a house on Lydos, a few detached, faded Hebrew letters float on its pale yellow surface, as if they had escaped from a painting by Chagall, who visited Vilna in the 1920s and 1930s when Jewish culture was flourishing.

These detached Hebrew letters, the flower from Ponary and the floating, carved Star of David are metaphors for the 80,000 Jewish souls from this charming, prosperous town executed by the Nazis. They hover over the city, and spoke to me every day I was there. I hear them still, their voices rustling like leaves in a high wind, like notes in the most poignant symphony ever played.

Memorial at Ponary.

Ponary today.

Music is portrayed in the documentary made by my dear friend Mira van Doren, a gifted filmmaker, Vilnaite, and Vilna Authority. Her newly released classic, *The World Was Ours*, about prewar Jewish cultural Vilna, is a moving commentary about the period when Vilna's Jewish artistic and cultural life flourished until the Nazis took power. In a conversation, we talked about why she made the film, and why I chose to put together these memoirs.

She suggested to me that whereas her purpose had been to honor history, mine was specifically to honor my parents, who had been integral members of that Jewish cultural cadre. And it was also to showcase the stories of two individuals who found themselves at a horrifying historical juncture facing unbearable pain, death, and loss. Graced with musical talent that guided them on the path of survival, they, their family members, and others in their doomed community utilized their innate gifts to uplift the shattered lives of their fellow-Jews. They inspire us with their example and demonstrate that it is infinitely more beneficial, satisfying, and constructive to build, grow, and achieve goals directed toward higher levels of the human spirit.

So, what were our personal quests, Mira's and mine? We were simply saying, "Thank you" to our families. Thank you for providing a legacy that celebrated life.

Thank you, Max and Fania, for being dignified, utterly decent, caring human beings, loving parents, and proud, tender guardians of such pain-filled memory. Thank you for giving me life and, by your example, for putting me on a path of honor, respect, and love for my people and our world.

The music goes on.

Gallery

Caricature by H. Marty inscribed, "To my friend Beker, a
remembrance of a good friendship," Görlitz, 1941.

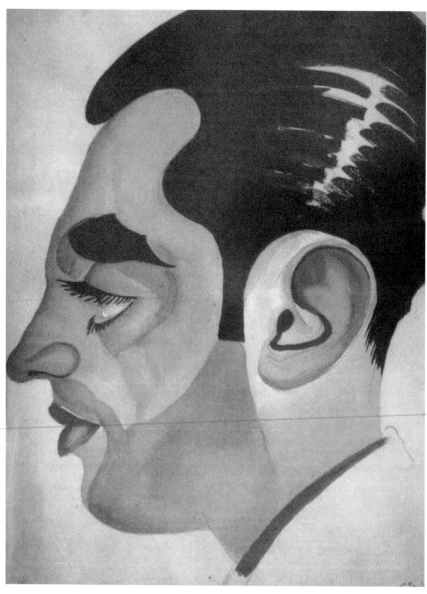

Poster of my father, Max Beker, by Henrot.
March 1941.

Pen and ink drawing of Max Beker by B. Thomato.
"With all my admiration and good wishes to Monsieur Beker
for the talent of a great violinist."
August 4, 1941.

Sonia Beker watercolor done by Max Beker's fellow POW
H. Marty from a photo (see pg. 77 & 97).

Sonia Beker's image scratched onto shellacked wooden
cigarette box lid done by another fellow POW.
Also from same photo (see pg. 77).

The DP Orchestra. Max (far right) with Fania (in front of him).

Fania and Max after Liberation.

Fania and Henia Durmashkin.

A visa to go to Israel was soon followed by an order to report
to the Israeli army.

The Jewish Orchestra members and friends, 1949.

Akiva Durmashkin
"More about Yosselle Rosenblatt, Of Blessed Memory"
The Shul and the Cantorial World (November 1937)
(English translation from Yiddish by Lazer Mishulovin
YIVO Library Archive)

Yoselle Rosenblatt belonged to the old style of *Chazanim* (cantors); throughout his whole life he was artistically productive. Unlike Rabbi Nissen Belzer o.b.m. or Zeidel Rovner, whose compositions were of the old standard with little musical tact, and phrases lacking harmonious form. Rosenblatt's creations are also Jewish, but his music was with form. His *"B'tziet Yisroal"* would evoke great ecstasy from the Vilna audience. His *"U'vnucho Yomar," "Hal'le'lu Avdai,"* his *"Birchat Kohanim,"* his *"V'al Kulom",* his *"Yismachu,"* his *"V'shamru,"* which he sent me not long before his death; his pearls in our synagogal music-literature, his *"V'af hu haya mitkaven"* used to inspire the Vilna worshippers.

I remember the following episode: When I was standing at the *amud* (synagogal lectern) with the Chazan Moshe Kosovitzky in the Great Synagogue of Vilna on Yom Kippur during the *avoda* services and we were singing the *"V'af hu haya mitkaven,"* composed by Yosselle Rosenblatt, requests were heard from the worshippers: "Sing it again, and again; we are ready to stay late into the night, if only to hear these heart-inspiring compositions sung."

Yoselle's being, his appearance, his personality! It was a true pleasure to spend time with him. Every organ of his body exuded authentic Jewish purity and religion. Everyone sings his creations, but he only sings a small percent of others'; for the most part, he used to sing his own creations. Not to mention his recitatives, which have no equal in the Chazanut world. There is yet to be born one who can fully carry out his own creation in a performance. Who possesses his soft tone, his minor scale, his middle scale and his wonderful falsetto with the coloratura? It was something supernatural. His ordinary *k'naitchele* (nuances), his *k'rechts* (cry) with the opening of his mouth. . .

I will never forget the impression that he made on me when I was standing with him at the Vilner *amud* on an ordinary weekly *maariv* (evening services), when he began to deal with the prayer-text, seemingly with the ordinary *nusach* (prayer-version), but his prayer tore apart my heart. His tamboura and the colossal metallic vibration of his tone were so tightly bonded and stitched with his Jewish prayer and with the aesthetic prayer dialect, that the blood in my veins began to flow with tempo and I totally lost myself.

His *"V'hu Rachum,"* which he sent, for me to sing together with the choir, he created while he was sitting in a wagon. In a conversation that I had with him, he once told me that many of his compositions were created while walking in the street. The man was literally unable to walk around unoccupied, inactive, not creating.

He was the true example of "Know before whom you stand."[*] We live today in such bitter and harsh times that no one seems to give any "judgement and accounting"[*] in the concept of the "service of God"; not the congregants nor the "congregation's emissaries" (cantors). We are very far and perhaps totally detached from the concept of "Know before whom you stand" and sometimes the survivor buries his head in shame and silence because no one will hear him and no one wants to understand him.

A few years ago, I wrote an open letter in the Vilna *Tog* (Daily) where I thanked Yosselle and wished him from the depths of my heart that he should merit singing his heart-inspiring prayers in Jerusalem; and the blessing was actually fulfilled. When they heard him praying in Israel, the audiences were amazed by his sweet prayers that touched the heart of the listener. However, that he should die in Israel–that I didn't gather! We simple people, when we die, they place in our graves a small sack of earth from the Land of Israel. Yoselle, however, merited by the Master of the Universe that his entire body be buried in the earth of our Holy Land of Israel.

---

[*]A verse from Ethics of Our Fathers, Chapter 3, Mishna 1 that is posted on the synagogal lectern and is also a classical cantorial score composed by Yosselle Rosenblatt.

Letter from my great-uncle Wulf Beker to his sister, Lisa Baker.

Vilna, 22/2 1940

Beloved sister and brother-in-law,

A long time has passed since I last wrote to you. I am certain that you, my beloved sister, are distressed over it, but now is not the time to talk about it, because, after such a lengthy time, you should receive happier letters and be prouder of me. But unfortunately, I have come to you now with fresh and sad news.

It is, by now, six months since the war broke out and all of the misfortunes that fell upon us. You know indeed, our beloved sister, we lived through very bad times from the war and hunger and, unfortunately, we are now left in a very critical situation.

For a few months, I was fighting with myself not to write you concerning all of this. However, beloved sister, you know quite well that besides you, I have no one in this world to whom I can express my bitter heart. I am certain that you will understand me very well and, as much as possible, help me out in our needy circumstances.

Beloved sister, with the break of war I became totally ruined, physically and materially. In Poland I had [work] and now with the breakdown of Poland, I am broken down. I lost my job and I am left without any opportunities to make a living.

It is already six months that I am suffering along with my whole family and I have nowhere to turn. I hope, beloved sister, you will understand my letter very well and help me in my desperate situation as much as possible and with your whole heart.

I am ending off my writing, beloved sister, and I wish that my letter will find you in a good time. May the beloved God grant you to be able to help us with our needs.

Regards and hearty kisses to you and your whole family,

Your brother,

Wulf

My wife Dobi and children send you all their hearty regards.

I beg of you, beloved sister, write to me how you are living. Do you have any livelihood? Any *nachas* from your beloved children? I will be very happy to hear good news from you as well. How is your beloved husband, my brother-in-law Kusial? Is he healthy? Can he work?

Letter from my grandfather, Boris Beker to his sister, Lisa
Baker, in Brooklyn.

B. Bexeris.

Poplavsna g-ve 11-7

Vilnius.

Lietuvia

Beloved sister and brother-in-law!

We can write to you that we are, thank God, healthy. May we hear the same from you. Beloved sister and Brother-in-law, Our strength is expiring due to our extremely desperate situation and from the cold that is constantly with us. You are aware of the devastation that met us and in which we find ourselves. We were suffering with *tsuris* (troubles) before, but now it is an outcry. We have lost everything of our lives. Previously, I would receive retirement every Monday; it wasn't so much, but I had enough to pay the rent and for the wood for the winter. But now it is already the fifth month that I did not pay any rent and the landlord is *ripping my flesh*.

Although, these debts are not what concern me, I am anxious to find a way out of this hunger situation. We are, literally, expiring from hunger. If it will continue much longer, then our lives are over. We would not care, but the children, who have yet to taste life, will have to die from hunger and for them it will be a great loss.

In addition, the uncontrollable frost does not cease. We are suffering from so much cold; it is unbearable. We are left naked and barefoot. The children are not going to school because they are bare-naked.

In a word, beloved sister, the depressing circumstances that we find ourselves in is indescribable. I would have written to you long ago but, unfortunately, I don't have the means with which to buy a postage stamp. My oldest son, Leibe, brought extra postage and sat here until I wrote this letter.

Beloved sister, I don't mean to cause you any pain. My bitter need and situation pushes me to turn to you and, God knows the truth, that aside from you I have no one to turn to.

You have not forsaken me in the best of times. I hope, my beloved sister, that in these bitter times which we are living through, you will help me out and save me from hunger and from nakedness.

I would write to you in more detail, but not everything is allowed to be written, and in addition, I don't want to anger you. I have already written enough information that will give you no joy.

Beloved Lisa, I can write to you that Ethel came after so many years of not seeing each other. She spent four weeks here. She stayed at Simon's brother this time; since she didn't find any *nachas* with me once she saw my life and my situation. She was upset when she came to see us; to such a terrible extent she did not imagine our circumstances.   Besides, she thought that she was coming to rich brothers but found us in worse poverty than herself. She has already returned home and will write a letter from there. She doesn't look as old as her photo. She doesn't complain much; has her own house, manages the bath and survives. She is not making any big business but works and earns for her daily needs. Ethel herself has said that her life is easier than ours. She married off three children and the three younger ones live nearby. She would want to help me but, unfortunately, is in need of help herself.

Therefore, there is no *nachas* from anyone. Look at Chatzkel. He darkened his whole life in the army in order not to have to succumb to anyone in his old age. And now, he is left helpless. One month before the war broke out, he applied for retirement. He wasn't even eligible to receive one cent. All his sweat was for naught; everything went to the devil and he is left helpless just like me.

We are bitter and when I visit, I find him in the same situation as myself. Now, he realizes how badly he treated me in the period when he lived like a god in Odessa and did not feel my suffering and ignored me. Now, he acknowledges his wrongdoing towards me, since he has met with the same desperate fate. He was still not used to any hunger, so he didn't empathize with me. But when it pressured him, he feels the same as everyone.

However, I do not see it as any revenge, since I am in similar circumstances and even worse, since I have small children to support while he does not. Yet, it is a bitter pity on him. *He sleeps with one eye open.* In a word, my beloved sister, we all failed in everything.

Beloved sister, he will write you a letter. You should answer him. Let's forget about the past foolishness. Time has already shown and taught him that there is no ego and there is no I in this world, only humanity. That is above all. I told him to take you as an example and learn how to behave. Today, he acknowledges everything that I foretold him. Meanwhile, my beloved sister, his lot is very bad and bitter.

There is nothing to do and there is nowhere to turn and the need is great. I beg of you, beloved Lisa, see to send us help as soon as possible. There is, literally, nothing.

Over here, lots of help is being sent from American relatives. I hope that the happy day will come when we receive help from you. When the morning comes, I look out with eyes towards the postman, perhaps he will bring us the help that we are impatiently waiting for. But we are still stuck in the same *tsuris.*

Only one thing calms us; that is hope; the hope that we await in our desperate need and, furthermore, in such bitter times and with all of the suffering that we endure.

I know, my beloved sister, that you are trying to help us sooner and better, but we are waiting too long, because we are already burnt out. There are no words to describe our suffering. For once, all we want is to have a piece of bread to satisfy ourselves. We don't want any luxury, only bread to fill ourselves, that is all we need.

See to it, my sister, to help us as soon as possible, and save us from a definite hunger death

Be well.

Your brother Boris,

Regards to our beloved brother-in-law and uncle, Kusial; may he be well and have *nachas* from his children and grandchildren, lots of *nachas.* Also, regards to Max, Sonia and their family; may they be healthy and strong.

My wife and children send their greetings; may you all be healthy.

My son still has not returned from captivity.

Be well.

Please answer right away

B. Bekeris

Paupio Gatve 11-7

Vilnius, Lithuania

Letter from Boris Beker to his sister, Lisa Baker,
in Brooklyn, NY, September 25, 1941.

Vilnius, 25/9 41

Beloved sister and brother-in-law,

I can write to you that, thank God, we are healthy. May we hear the same from you.

Beloved sister, we don't know what to make of your silence. I wrote to you so many letters and I did not receive any response. I thought that in these times no letters are arriving to America, however, we received many other letters. The heart grieves seeing letters arriving but not from you. I cannot understand why? We don't care about anything; all we care about is how you are doing and about your health.

I cannot imagine that you, beloved sister, would be totally uninterested in our fate, if we are alive or not. After all that we went through until the entry of the Red Army who liberated us from all of the terror that we found ourselves in. [Now we are free and safe.]

Beloved Lisa, I beg of you, please have mercy on me and write to me how you are doing. How is your health? How are the children? In a word, write to me about everything in detail. After such a long silence, it is about time to hear how you are doing. I am sick from worrying. You can write freely. The letter will arrive. Perhaps a day earlier or a day later, but it will arrive. However, if you don't write then certainly no letter will arrive on time. I wrote to you so much, I sent you *"fresh air."* But until this very day, I have not received any word from you.

I hope that this time you will take upon yourself to write me a letter with great detail.

Beloved sister, I can write to you that my son is still in captivity. If only he would be home, I would not be worried at all, because he supported me with everything. Without him, it is not good. But we are constantly hoping that God will help and he will come back home.

My older daughter works. She earns not bad. The same is with my younger son. The rest are studying. In this manner, we are living and surviving. I am very happy about it. The main thing is that we are free and we don't have to be afraid to go on the bus. We are secure with our daily life and with everything; more than usual. We can purchase freely. No one holds us back; besides for health and money. I can write to you that Chatzkel is in the best of circumstances. His daughter married, six months ago, to a very fine and intelligent man and she lives very well with him. He is, indeed, a good man. Chatzkel does not deserve such a good son-in-law, after such behaviour and for the way he treated her. He took her as she is, but now she is a normal person. There is a lot to write about him, but I have my own *tsuris*, so it is not worth to involve myself with him. *"The way a man lies down, that is the way he sleeps."* Beloved Lisa, I ask you again, please respond right away and write to me about everything.

You, your husband and children should be well. May we hear from you only good news.

Best wishes from your brother, brother-in-law and uncle,

Boris

My wife and all of the children send you their hearty regards. May you be healthy and strong. Please answer right away.

This is my address:

B. Bekeris
Paupio Gatve 11-7
Vilnius
L.T.S.R.

If possible, please send us a package. It will arrive. I am in dire need of things.

Warszawa 3-go Stycznia 1939.

Letter from Moshe Koussevitsky to my
great-uncle, Mordechai Durmashkin

Letter from Moshe Koussevitsky (translation follows)

[Polish] 1939

Highly esteemed friend, Mr. Mordechai Durmashkin,

Naturally, you are wondering as to the reason why I am currently writing to you. However, evidently due to today's situation, when everyone's eyes are focused on your *Goldene* America in general, and to the good friends and relatives in America in particular, it is no wonder that I am writing.

In addition, I was in America last year and have tasted from the finest, but unfortunately, over here, we do not feel so at all. So why then the wonder?!

Indeed, I long for America and for the fortunate who have the opportunity to be there and benefit from all of the good feelings that we are missing here. In a word, we are yearning for all of this!

The hopeless situation for the Jews in Europe on the one hand, and the affable relations that I have with your brother's son, Wolf Durmaskin, on the other hand, compels me to turn to you, my beloved friend, with this letter and the following request.

He is a frequent guest at our home and we are in a bonding friendship. He is my accompanist and we play together at the frequent concerts in the country, which is considered a rarity.

Anyone in America would wish for himself to be able to do this in general and in addition as a player and accompanist for concerts. This is a talent in the full sense of the word.

But what is worth all of the praises of his gifts, if here in Europe it is not being utilized correctly, and with time it can, Heaven forbid, vanish.

These sentiments and thoughts compelled me to write you to settle what we can do for him and be able to schlep him out of here. I don't want to list all of his virtues and the benefits, firstly for him, his family and relatives, and also perhaps for me as well. How do the Americans say "Once in America, always in America."

Sooner or later, I desire and plan to be with my family in America and he would be able to join me in my successes at all my concerts which I am scheduled to perform in the future. It is self-understood what this would mean for him, morally and materialistically.

I, from my end, cannot do anything because if I travel, I will have to travel as an immigrant. Only relatives can help him. Therefore, I suggest that you seize this opportunity and immediately begin to work on behalf of your very very talented and gifted nephew Wolf Durmashkin. According to the current situation, things are getting worse and worse; it will literally be considered a failure and a great loss for America.

In my opinion, he has a field of beneficial work for his whole family and for us singers/cantors.

Concerning the required forms for the American council, you can do it on your own, or, if you are unable, you can have a friend help you.

I hope it will provide you moral satisfaction, recognizing the calling of the time; and that the fruit from this work will be to the benefit of all of us and for the happiness of his family, relatives, and artists.

With hope that you will take heed of this letter and, if possible, already begin working. Don't procrastinate because it takes time to request a visa at the council and the quota is very strict.

I am finishing off my writing and I wish you all the best. With hope that the plans be speedily actualized.

With friendly regards to you and your esteemed family,

From me, your friend who honors you,

Moshe Koussevitzky
Cantor of Warsaw.

P.S. Please do not share with anyone what I wrote to you.

Notes

[1] Israel Cohen, *Vilna* (Phila., PA: The Jewish Publication Society, 1943), 1.

[2] Ellis Rivkin, *The Shaping of Jewish History* (New York: Scribner, 1971),

[3] Cohen, 105.

[4] Cohen, 310.

[5] Shmuel Spector and Geoffrey Wigoder, *The Encyclopedia of Jewish Life: Before and During the Holocaust* (Jerusalem: Yad Vashem, 2001), 1399.

[6] Cohen, 334.

[7] Cohen, 337.

[8] Cohen, 339.

[9] Cohen, 351.

[10] Cohen, 345.

[11] Cohen, 346.

[12] Cohen, 358.

[13] Cohen, 361.

[14] Cohen, 372.

[15] Spector and Wigoder, 1400.

[16] Cohen, 389.

[17] Cohen, 389.

[18] Cohen, 401.

[19] Cohen, 402.

[20] Cohen, 405; Spector and Wigoder, 1400.

[21] Cohen, 406.

[22] Cohen, 413; Spector and Wigoder, 1400.

[23] Spector and Wigoder, 1400.

[24] Herman Kruk, *The Last Days of the Jerusalem of Lithuania: Chronicles from the Vilna Ghetto and the Camps, 1939-1944,* trans. by Barbara Harshav (New York: YIVO Institute for Jewish Research, 2002), xliii.

[25] Cohen, 420.

[26] Kruk, xxxix.

[27] Kruk, xxxix; Spector and Wigoder, 1401.

[28] Spector and Wigoder, 1401.

[29] Spector and Wigoder, 1401.

[30] Sima Skurkovitz, *Sima's Songs: Light in Nazi Darkness* (Jerusalem: Christian Friends of Israel, 1993), 9.

[31] N. N. Shneidman, *Jerusalem of Lithuania: The Rise and Fall of Jewish Vilnius* (New York: Mosaic Press Publishers, 1998), 47.

[32] Skurkovitz, 9.

[33] Skurkovitz, 18.

[34] Shneidman, 59.

[35] Shneidman, 59.

[36] Shneidman, 59.

[37] Shneidman, 60.

[38] Narrative by Stefan Luscevic.

[39] Rachel Kostanian-Danzig, *Spiritual Resistance in the Vilna Ghetto* (Vilna: Vilna Gaon Jewish State Museum), 112.

[40] Spector and Wigoder, 1402; Kruk, xlvii.

[41] Shneidman, 61.

[42] Shneidman, 64.

[43] Shneidman, 66-67.

[44] Spector and Wigoder, 1403; Kostanian-Danzig, 76.

[45] Shneidman, 67.

[46] Kostanian-Danzig, 64.

[47] Kostanian-Danzig, 65.

[48] Spector and Wigoder, 1402.

[49] Kostanian-Danzig, 22-23.

[50] Kruk. xlvi.

[51] Kruk. xlvii.

[52] Spector and Wigoder, 1403.

[53] The Database of Jewish Communities: Jewish Community of Vilna; The Solly Yellin Center of Lithuanian Jewry; http://www.bh.org.il/Communities/Archive/Vilna.asp, 8, 9.

[54] The Database of Jewish Communities: Jewish Community of Vilna

[55] The Database of Jewish Communities: Jewish Community of Vilna

[56] Narrative by Stefan Luscevic, tour guide of Vilna and Jewish Vilna.

[57] Cantor Natan Stolnitz, "Akiva Durmashkin and His

Influence on Liturgical Music in Old Radom," *The Radomer Voice*, April 1964.

[58] Stolnitz.

[59] Stolnitz.

[60] Stolnitz.

[61] Stolnitz.

[62] Stolnitz.

[63] Stolnitz.

[64] Stolnitz.

[65] Stolnitz.

[66] Kostanian-Danzig, 87.

[67] Kostanian-Danzig, 88.

[68] Kostanian-Danzig, 88.

[69] Stolnitz.

[70] Stolnitz.

[71] *Vilnius Ghetto: List of Prisoners, Vol. 1* (New York: Jewish Museum, 1996), 305; Narrated by Regina Kopilevich, Guide of Jewish Vilna and Genealogist.

[72] Kostanian-Danzig, 66.

[73] *Vilnius Ghetto: List of Prisoners, Vol. 1,* 271, 336.

[74] Alex Grobman, "American Jewish Chaplains and the Shearit Hapletah: April-June 1945" (Museum of Tolerance Online Multimedia learning Center; Annual 1 Chapter 05), pps. 1-9; http://motlc.wiesenthal.com/site/ pp.asp?c=gvKVLcMVluG&b=394979.

[75] Grobman.

[76] Grobman.

[77] Grobman.

[78] Grobman.

[79] Grobman.

[80] Grobman.

[81] Grobman.

[82] Robert L. Hilliard, *Surviving the Americans: The Continued Struggle of the Jews After Liberation* (Seven Stories Press, 1997), 41.

[83] Hilliard, 49.

[84] Grobman.

[85] Hilliard, 7.

[86] Hilliard, 8-10.
[87] Hilliard, 77.
[88] Hilliard, 188.
[89] Narrative by Jascha Gurewitz.
[90] Henny Gurko-Durmashkin, "Songs to Remember," from *Anthology on Armed Jewish Resistance 1939-1945* by Issac Kowalski (Brooklyn, NY: Jewish Combatants Pub House, 1984).
[91] Joan Peyser, *Bernstein, A Biography* (New York: Beech Tree Books, 1987), 399-400.

Bibliography

Books

Ben-Asher, Shlomo. *Legacy Interrupted: Yad Vashem – The Holocaust Martyrs' and Heroes' Remembrance Authority.* Jerusalem: "Art Plus," 2003.

Cohen, Israel. *Vilna.* Phila., PA: The Jewish Publication Society, 1992.

Cohen, Richard. *The Avengers: A Jewish War Story.* New York: First Vintage Books, 2001.

Ehrenburg, Ilya and Vasily Grossman, eds. *The Black Book.* New York: Yad Vashem & Israel Research Institute of Contemporary Society, 1980.

Gurko-Durmashkin, Henny. "Songs to Remember," from *Anthology on Armed Jewish Resistance 1939-1945* by Issac Kowalski. Brooklyn, NY: Jewish Combatants Pub House, 1984.

Hilliard, Robert L. *Surviving the Americans: The Continued Struggle of the Jews after Liberation.* New York: Seven Stories Press, 1997.

Katzurginsky, Shmerke *Churban Vilna.*

Kostanian-Danzig, Rachel. *Spiritual Resistance in the Vilna Ghetto.* Vilnius: The Vilna Gaon Jewish State Museum, 2004.

Kruk, Herman. *The Last Days of the Jerusalem of Lithuania: Chronicles from the Vilna Ghetto and the Camps, 1939-1944,* translated by Barbara Harshav. New York: Yad Vashem & Israel Research Institute of Contemporary Society, 2002.

Levin, Dov. *The Litvaks: A Short History of the Jews in Lithuania.* Jerusalem: Yad Vashem, 2001.

Peyser, Joan. *Bernstein, A Biography.* New York: Beech Tree Books, 1987.

Skurkovitz, Sima. *Sima's Songs: Light in Nazi Darkness.* Jerusalem: Christian Friends of Israel, 1993.

Shneidman, N. N. *Jerusalem of Lithuania: The Rise and Fall of Jewish Vilnius, A Personal Perspective*. Buffalo, NY: Mosaic Press, 1998.

Spector, Shmuel and Geoffrey Wigoder, *The Encyclopedia of Jewish Life: Before and During the Holocaust*. Jerusalem: Yad Vashem, 2001.

Vilna Ghetto Posters: Jewish Spiritual Resistance. Vilnius: The Vilna Gaon Jewish State Museum, 1999.

Vilnius Ghetto: List of Prisoners, Vol. 1. Vilnius: The Vilna Gaon Jewish State Museum, 1996.

Articles

Durmashkin, Akiva. "More about Yosselle Rosenblatt, Of Blessed Memory," *The Shul and the Cantorial World* (November 1937) (English translation from Yiddish by Lazer Mishulovin YIVO Library Archive)

Grobman, Alex; "American Jewish Chaplains and the Shearit Hapletah: April-June 1945"; Museum of Tolerance ONLINE Multimedia Learning Center. http://motlc.wiesenthal.com/site/pp.asp?c=gvKVLcMVluG&b=394979

"Jewish Community of Vilna"; The Solly Yellin Center of Lithuanian Jewry; The Database of Jewish Communities; Museum of the Jewish People; The Nahum Goldmann Museum Of the The Jewish Diaspora; http://www.bh.org.il/Communities/Archive/Vilna.asp.

Stolnitz, Cantor Natan; "Akiva Durmashkin and His Influence on Liturgical Music in Old Radom." *Radomer Shtime*, 1964.

"The Central Committee of the Liberated Jews (1945-1950)"; Jewish Virtual Library, The American-Israeli Cooperative Enterprise. http://www.jewishvirtuallibrary.org/jsource/holocaust/centralcomm.html.

"The Future Began at the DP- Camp Landsberg; Camps in the Landsberg Area During the Last Year of the War"; Landsberg im 20. Jahrhundert; Burgervereinigung; http://

www.buerger vereinigung-landsberg.org/english/dpcamp/
dp_camp.shtml.

Films

Michalczyk, John. *Displaced! Miracle at St. Ottilien,* 2002.
    -----*Creating Harmony: The Displaced Persons Orchestra at St.
    Ottilien,* 2007
Van Doren, Mira. *The World Was Ours,* 2006.